Avery Press
New York • London

The Courage to Be Courageous © 2022 by Dan Bolen and
Landon J. Napoleon.

This book is a work of nonfiction. In most cases, the author uses pseudonyms to protect the anonymity and privacy of actual people. All rights reserved, including the right of reproduction in whole or in part in any form. No part of this book may be used or reproduced by any means, graphic, electronic or mechanical, including photocopying, recording, taping or by any information storage retrieval system without the written permission of the author, except in the case of brief quotations in critical articles and reviews.

ISBN 978-1-7348774-5-8

Cover design by Sarah Cook Design.

Manufactured in the United States of America.

The Courage to Be Courageous

a memoir
of struggle, success, and truth

DAN BOLEN
With **LANDON J. NAPOLEON**

Dedicated to anyone out there who's still struggling to embrace the truth of who they are.

Author's Note

IN WRITING THIS MEMOIR, I'VE MADE EVERY attempt to be accurate. However, my primary source is my own memory stretching back across more than seventy years. Memories, of course, are an imperfect record, but my intention has been pure. On these pages are my best recollections that shaped who I am.

Above all else, I've tried to be rigorously honest, mindful, and transparent while also protecting the identity of anyone who didn't ask to be in this book. To protect the privacy of those depicted, I have changed names (except in a few cases where I received permission to use real names), locations, and identifying characteristics.

Prologue

Cleveland, Ohio, May 17, 2021

WHEN YOU'RE 73 AND YOU LAND IN CLEVELAND, U.S.A., two things are going to happen. First, you're going to the Rock & Roll Hall of Fame. And then, the next day, you're coming here for the third time: to the renowned Cleveland Clinic, where the cardiologist tells you to go ahead and live your life as you have been (but don't lift anything over thirty pounds), but figure that in one year you're going to need open heart surgery.

With that kind of news, I'd rather be back at the Rock Hall admiring the Prince exhibit. Prince Rogers Nelson once said, "You can always tell when the groove is working or not." Well, the groove that's not working in my heart is that I have a bicuspid valve instead of a tricuspid valve. At this writing in 2021, my aorta is expanding and that valve—with two flaps instead of three—

is leaking. Like I said: I'd rather be blissfully immersed back at the Rock Hall. Prince, who was a Jehovah's Witness, also said, "Religion is good except when it starts interfering with the rights of other people." Looking back at my life, I would have to agree. I was both religious and negatively affected by that same religion.

This trip unfolds at the tail end of the global COVID-19 pandemic, so the Hyatt Regency at Arcade was eerily vacant upon my arrival May 15. Then off to see Prince the next day, and now here today. Before seeing the cardiologist, they drew my blood for testing and administered an echocardiogram and MRI. Then the cardiologist used technical specifications to establish his prognosis, a measurement of the ascending aorta in centimeters. The surgery to repair my aorta and replace the valve requires ten days of post-op in the hospital and, God willing, full recovery in six weeks. Back to that valve replacement: they would use either a bovine valve, a pig valve, or a titanium valve, which means I would potentially either moo, oink, or clank.

The potential for open heart surgery makes you ponder things—life, death, and everything in between, including the career you chose and the things you sacrificed along the way. Important things that went by the wayside, time after time.

Don't lift anything over thirty pounds.

Well, then, that's not really living my life because, even in my seventies, I'm in the gym six days a week. I guess it runs in the family (not the Jack LaLanne lifestyle, but rather heart disease). Both my parents died from heart issues. My younger brother Dean died at age 59 in Mexico after a heart attack and stroke. My older brother Lee suffered several serious strokes and had open heart surgery. My sister Sue had a stroke. Including my sister Marie, five of us seven Bolen children had holes in our hearts. And the doctors told us that such holes in the heart aren't hereditary!

Tomorrow I go home to Arizona to live my life the way I have been… except without lifting anything over thirty pounds. But that limitation won't stick, because I'm a workout animal. To add to my anxiety, the surgeon says there's a forty percent chance I may not need the surgery at all in the next ten years. I prefer to live in that forty percent, with the surgeon's support, and keep lifting weights six days a week. Along with my one hour of cardio each day. The medical confusion leaves me feeling like so many others in the heat of two different diagnoses: frustrated, out of control, and vulnerable.

That kind of vulnerability has ways of opening doors inside yourself. Exhibit One: When you use dysfunction to run your life, there's always a payoff. And, boy did I dysfunction my way through this lifetime. Prince also said, "Sometimes it takes years for a person to become an overnight success."

My overall financial success took half a century, even though I made my first million when I was in my early thirties. I'm not saying that to impress anyone; I was never driven by money, but by a love of what I did. I love people. I'm motivated by helping people. While those traits catapulted me to the top of my profession, there was a downside, too, which is that I have the "disease to please." That's my default. I mention the money because in my trust I've already earmarked a sum for Cleveland Clinic to continue the important work they do to change and save people's lives, including pioneering medical breakthroughs such as the first face transplant in the United States—and my possible coronary surgery.

I piled up all the external markers: house, wife, family, church leader, and lifestyle. But I only began finding my true success at age 70—a deeper and more important success rooted in transparency and honesty, which finally led me to total peace—it's never too late. Except now the mortality clock is ticking a bit more loudly, with a potential major heart surgery looming.

Money is great—no doubt—but now I realize I don't want to die with any secrets, including all the old family stuff I've been covering up all these years. I was fearful, hidden, and voiceless for seven decades. Now I want my story to be heard. I'm actually excited by the specter of truth-telling, because vulnerability also can bring peace. For the record, I'm equally terrified by the vulnerability this process engenders.

Welcome to my world: a lifetime rolling on the twin tracks of high energy and dark terror.

Part 1
Struggle

One

Boise, Idaho, 1969

"I WANT THAT DESK."

June Wells seemed perplexed by my directness. She scowled slightly, glanced at the empty desk across the office, and then back at me. "That's our training desk."

"I'll work there," I said, smiling broadly.

She eyed me again, suspiciously. A developing smoker's rasp hardened her authority when she said, "We have no openings."

"I would like that desk," I said again, as resolute and plainly as if I were asking for cream with my coffee. She, too, had just been direct with me, so her confusion was understandable: I had showed up here at the employment agency Snelling and Snelling trying to conjure a job in my off-the-rack blue suit from Sears, Roebuck and Company, an organization I was desperately attempting to re-designate from my "current" to "previous" employer.

June Wells was pushing 50, I guessed, with an olive complexion and a jet-black bouffant hairdo spiraling upward toward the white panel ceiling.

"What do you want to do here?" she asked.

"I'm here to work."

"We don't have any openings."

"You have a desk over there," I said again, pointing like a child at a full gumball machine.

She started to respond and then caught herself, not wanting to get pulled back into my *Who's On First?* loop again. She narrowed her gaze: "What *exactly* are you doing here?"

"I'm here to work. I want that desk."

In 1969, Snelling and Snelling was the largest employment agency in the United States. I had come here to Boise, unsolicited, on my day off from selling men's clothes at Sears, to seek a job with a better upward trajectory. If this was the biggest operation in the game of putting people to work, whether in accounting, clerical, technical, or sales jobs, it wasn't overly impressive at first glance. But if it was indeed at the top of the food chain, then it was where I wanted to be. The small open room I could see had eight desks, including the training desk she had mentioned. They were separated by five-foot glass dividers, including that open training desk I would soon be occupying. The sales motivator Zig Ziglar gives the best description of my unbreakable spirit on that cool April day: *You don't have to be great to start, but you have to start to be great.* Hallelujah.

There were seven people at the other seven desks, all hard at work, and all but one was smoking a cigarette. Three were women, who were all in dresses or skirts—as required, I assumed.

"Well, Mr…"

"Bolen. Dan Bolen."

"Right. You'll have to talk to our manager." June Wells was done trying to unravel my ulterior motives.

"What's her name?"

"Lynn Haynes."

"I'd like to talk to her, please."

"You'll need to make an appointment. She's *extremely* busy."

Over the next fifty-plus years of making hundreds of thousands of phone calls, I would learn some immutable facts, one of which was that every single person in the U.S. workforce was, at any given moment of the work day, either "very busy," "extremely busy," "in a meeting," or simply "unavailable." No one was ever bored, looking for something to do, killing time by the water cooler, or open to a lively chat to whittle away some time before lunch.

"Is she here?" I asked.

"Who?"

"Lynn Haynes," I said, as though Lynn and I were pals from way back.

June Wells eyed me again and made the calculation that this was her chance to pass me off to her boss. "Wait here, please," she said, before getting up and disappearing into the smoke haze and beyond.

Before I had come here to Snelling and Snelling, I had deployed an even more militarized job-hunting strategy. That approach started with a job interview to be a personnel assistant at Intermountain Gas Company. I was 21, with no college degree, because I'd dropped out at the not-so-subtle behest of my religion (more on that later), and didn't have much to offer Intermountain Gas Company beyond a pleasant smile, my stellar personality, a great sense of humor, and a driving work ethic that would embarrass an eight-oxen plow team. I had my father to credit for my work mettle, courtesy of three things he did throughout my childhood: ignore me, beat me, and teach me how to work.

The woman who interviewed me and was the gatekeeper to my lucrative career as a personnel assistant, a job title that was not entirely clear to me, was a pleasant person in her sixties who tried to hide her dentures when she smiled.

"Thank you, Mr. Bolton," she said, standing to shake my hand and covering her mouth with her other hand. "We'll let you know in two weeks."

"It's Bolen. Dan Bolen."

"OK, you have a nice day."

"Is there anything else I can do to show my interest in this position?" I said.

She just shook her head. "I'm not sure I... but we'll let you know."

I thanked her and left. Standing by idly, however, while the denture lady toyed with my ticket out of men's retail at Sears, was simply not in the Dan Bolen playbook. Instead I started to follow Zig Ziglar's encouragement to be great, somehow, in the days when rotary dial telephones and No. 2 pencils were high technology, by tracking down where my interviewer lived. Luckily for me, this was a different era and more than twenty years before California became the first state to enact a specific stalking statute. On a sunny Saturday morning, before Sears opened, I put on my blue suit and tie, as always, and knocked on the front door of her house. Before she had even fully opened the door I was off and running.

"Hi, I'm Dan Bolen," I said, smiling and extending my hand. "Good to see you."

She was clutching at the lapels of her pink bathrobe with wild hair twirled in every direction. She narrowed the gap between the door and the jamb and said, "I don't know you."

"Sure, you do. You interviewed me for the personnel assistant job."

She only paused briefly before slamming the door without saying another word. That was the abrupt extinction of my illustrious career as a personnel assistant at Intermountain Gas Company. With that experience in mind, when I showed up unannounced here at Snelling and Snelling, I was pleased that I had actually dialed back my persistence level at least to the point of knowing I would only be encountering people who were at a workplace during business hours and not still in their pajamas. But beyond that slight modification, Dan Bolen only knew one way forward.

Full speed. *Start to be great!* With a kind smile and gentle demeanor softening an unfailing determination.

I decided right then, before my dear friend Lynn Haynes

walked out with her similarly towering bouffant hairdo, which was bleach-blonde with a high wave on one side that made me tilt my head when I talked to her, that I would soon be Snelling and Snelling's top producer.

Two

Go-Go Boots that Blew My Mind

I GOT MARRIED TO HAVE SEX. AS A RELIABLE Jehovah's Witness (JW)—the same orthodoxy that quietly persuaded me to stop my college education altogether—I couldn't have sex without first getting married. I had been a horny teenager and an even hornier young adult, because, well, we weren't even allowed to take things into our own hands. Something had to give. When I saw the first future Mrs. Dan Bolen, she came striding into my father's grocery store in Palmer, Alaska, in knee-length, white go-go boots that blew my mind. I was working the bakery counter when she casually walked up and introduced herself.

"I'm Eileen," she said confidently. "I'm Walter Keaton's sister." Sure, I knew Walter Keaton, but holy cow, was his sister beautiful. I was looking for a woman, and she for a man. As I said, my personal situation was untenable. I was a powder keg ready to explode, and here was Eileen King, my potential lit match. I didn't care that she'd already been married and divorced by age

19. I wouldn't have cared if she had eleven toes and didn't speak English. Blame it on male hard-wiring, the white go-go boots, and her gorgeous smile. *Yes, yes, I do!*

I was 21 when we got married on February 24, 1968, in Kingdom Hall; it was a union that would last twenty-six years. She was a JW, too, so when we got back to the Captain Cook Hotel in Anchorage, after the wedding festivities, there would be no oral sex per church rules. I'd tried oral sex when I was 13, my only other sexual experience up to this moment. With third base off the table, I started at second base by feeling her breasts, which was dizzying terrain for a celibate young man. We then ran straight to home plate for the main act, which was my first time in such terrain. Oddly, the first time with my beautiful new wife was immensely pleasurable, at least from a valve-relief perspective, but not mind-shattering. I knew I was already in deep denial about why that was.

Thus began my new married life. We lived in Anchorage where we rented a small apartment. She was a waitress at Safeway, and I worked at my dad's second grocery store in Anchorage. All combined, we were pretty much flat broke. And while Eileen was a knockout in her white go-go boots (and any other footwear she chose), I did not yet know medical experts would diagnosis her as borderline, bipolar, and highly addictive.

In 1969 we moved from Anchorage to Meridian, Idaho, where we rented a small farmhouse out on Victory Road for eighty dollars a month. We would live there for the next ten years. I tried to build a small brick fireplace, which was a disastrous fiasco and my first and last home improvement project. I ended up taking off my pants, which were loaded with cement, and finishing the job in my white boxers. After this disaster, I quickly went into retail working full-time at Sears.

I'd had such a bad experience with my own father that I did not want to have children. The church doctrine was also not pro-children, as opposed to what one might have thought. Apparently, we in the JW faith were too busy preparing for end times and the battle of Armageddon to be challenged by the demands of child-rearing. I did, however, want to practice the first step of procreation with my new young wife, as much as she'd allow, as though we were trying to conceive… which of course we soon did. Sadly, Eileen had a miscarriage, and then another one. We soon conceived again and prayed that the third time would be the charm.

When I told my mom we were pregnant again, she had an odd response.

"So are we!"

Mom's declaration prompted an offspring's common thought, and slight nausea: *They still do it?*

Oddly, my older brother Lee's wife was also pregnant, producing a family triumvirate of expecting women who all went to the same Dr. Hume. They each had a new baby girl, born in the same hospital: I got a new daughter, a new sister, and a new niece in the span of ninety days. Our daughter Tiffany was born June 22, 1969, at St. Luke's Hospital in Boise.

A new child was the powerful impetus that led me, unsolicited, to my new/old friend Lynn Haynes—because, with a family of three, I desperately needed to up my income. Before securing another job, I went to Sears and gave my notice. And for the first time ever, my manager and I agreed on something, which was that I didn't need to stick around the men's department at Sears for another two weeks.

"What are you doing here?" Lynn Haynes asked.

"I'm here for the job." She had no idea who she was dealing with now.

"But we didn't advertise a job."

"I already quit my other job. I can work at that desk, which is empty."

The boldness play worked: Lynn Haynes relented to my confidence assault and hired me on the spot. New job in hand, I dived into my work at Snelling and Snelling, which was the beginning of a fifty-year career, the one that would earn me my first million in my thirties.

At Snelling and Snelling, that empty desk I had eyed at my ambush interview was now occupied by one Dan Bolen, in shirt and tie as required. Likewise, as I'd correctly suspected, the women were not allowed to wear trousers. The company placed enticing classified advertisements in the Idaho Statesman: *Now hiring salesmen at top pay! Two years' experience preferred. Call Dan Ray.*

Since Snelling and Snelling paid the newspaper by the letter for each job posting, we recruiters had to choose a short pseudonym. At work I was officially "Dan Ray." Most of our job placements were applicant-paid fees. Almost all the people who got jobs through us had to use their own credit card, or pay us in installments. My top fee of $1,200 was my first employer-paid fee, which we rarely got, from Boise Cascade for an accountant job. That was a big chunk of cash in 1969. My job was a daily whirlwind that suited me perfectly.

I determined it took about ten phone calls to get an applicant in front of an employer for an interview. Sometimes I used the Yellow Pages to find and call employers. I made fifty or more SOD calls per day ("spin of the dial," since we used rotary-dial telephones) to schedule five people to interview with prospective employers. We called these "SOs," or "send-outs," which meant we'd successfully gotten the applicant out on an interview. Fifty or more times each day I dialed and said, *Hello, this is Dan Ray with Snelling and Snelling, and I have an excellent candidate for your company to hear about today. Let me tell you what makes him so outstanding (and then give them a grabber!). Would you be interested in interviewing him at two o'clock today, or would four be better?* I made offers no one could refuse. If someone I was calling hung up on me, I would repeatedly call back.

"You hung up on me," I'd always say calmly. "Did we get cut off?" If they hung up again I called back and said, "That's really rude, and you won't get to hear about this outstanding candidate, who I was going to present to you first today; now it's necessary to present him to your competitor!" I thought it was important to maintain a sense of self-protection and dignity.

Lynn Haynes, who was in her sixties, lorded over the busy hub of activity. Lynn was a tough boss who hewed to the "my way or the highway" school of management. She'd leave during the day to get her hair re-piled toward the sky. She was demanding and funny. And hardcore. But since I was grinding out more calls in the smoke haze than anyone on any given day, we got along famously.

As I pledged before even starting, within three months I was the top performer at Snelling and Snelling, placing up to twelve people a month in new jobs. Besides the people who responded to our classified ads and came to our office, other applicants sometimes showed up unsolicited, just as I had done. I always admired the pluck in those applicants. June Wells did, too, and would tease me by saying *Two Dan Bolens waiting in the lobby.* If there was a woman, she would modify it to *There's a Danielle Bolen when you get a chance.* However, the unsolicited often had to sit and wait for hours before one of us could get to them; we were required to get a send-out with a company for each applicant before we moved on to the next person to interview.

Meanwhile, along with all the SOD calls and paperwork to process new applicants, we were each responsible for collections, as well. That is, we had to shake down people to collect the applicant-paid fee we'd earned. And if you failed on that front, the cheery Lynn Haynes was on you, with her Marlboro cigarette glowing, like ugly on an ape.

Husband, father, and now Snelling and Snelling's top recruiter at age 21. I was so busy I never had the time or space to ponder how, or why, I had such an unrelenting drive to succeed. What I did know was that I had discovered the passion of my life, and when I found my passion (placing people) I knew I would ultimately be successful regardless of the extreme odds. To more fully understand that would take us back to the beginning to my hardscrabble father—the man who would have killed me if he'd known the truth.

Three

Never Give Up Being You

LOOKING BACK, MY FATHER WAS A MAN I NEVER liked; rather, I felt obligated to love him because he was my dad. The one thing I remember clearly is he never touched me except when he was hitting me. That is, he never hugged or held me. In fact, I barely remember my dad ever talking to me much, either. He may have done those things, but I just can't remember. I don't remember any affection from my dad because he was mostly working all the time, and we rarely saw him.

His name was Benny Lee Bolen, but he went by Ben. He was born in Cape Fair, Missouri, and grew up there in the southern part of the state, one of nine kids with parents who were sharecroppers who worked in the fields and harvested fruit trees and other crops. He was six feet tall, slim, had thick, dark, wavy hair, and always wore a mustache. By any standard, he was very handsome. I saw photographs of him when he was in the U.S. Navy, and he looked like a model. Thankfully I got my dad's good looks, but not his charming personality!

That big brood of nine children (in order from oldest) included: Del, Clarence, Earl, Pauline, M (I can't remember the name, so we'll call her Auntie M), my father, Bonnie, Rayjean, and Dewey. I have fond memories of my Aunt Pauline, who was married to Harold and worked at Beauty Care Cosmetics in Boise, where she was a very successful sales representative and top district manager. She was outgoing and funny, and would dance with me. Sadly, Aunt Pauline and Auntie M both later suffered the horror of Alzheimer's. My Uncle Dewey was in the U.S. Merchant Marines; I may have seen him once in my life. I never knew what Uncle Dewey did, but it sounded important. I later learned that merchant mariners moved cargo and passengers between nations and within the United States, on all manner of waterborne craft, on oceans, the Great Lakes, rivers, canals, harbors, and other waterways. Indeed, it sounded like a great gig. My Uncle Earl was a bail bondsman, and my Aunt Rayjean worked at the Albertsons where my dad worked. Dad was actually the first manager at Joe Albertson's first store on State Street in Boise, Idaho. From there Albertsons became a national chain that today has more than 2,000 stores and 270,000 employees.

My father loved basketball, and he played for two different high schools in Meridian and Boise. Legend has it Ben Bolen was famous for his hook shot. At Meridian High School, Dad met my mother who, like Dad, was very attractive with her long, wavy auburn hair.

My mother, Mildred Howell, was born May 26, 1924, and grew up near Salt Lake City in a Mormon family. She had a tough upbringing, starting with the death of her mother when Mom was just 1. Her father was a schoolteacher and compulsive gambler. After the death of his wife, my maternal grandfather Orvid moved the family to Weston, Idaho, where he met and married a woman named Vera. She was a widow, with two boys from her first marriage, and had flaming red hair and wore high heels into her nineties. Grandma Vera would figure prominently in my own journey.

My maternal grandfather taught school most of his life, and was a heavy gambler. On paydays, after school he would stop by the pool hall and gamble away his paycheck. He was never able to get his gambling under control. Mom never really had a close relationship with her dad, and neither did we. When we visited to spend time with Grandma Vera, he was content to sit and watch television (he was quite good at *Jeopardy!*) while the rest of us would spend time with Grandma.

Mom had two siblings. My Aunt Helen grew up to have six boys in a row, before finally getting a girl with her last child. My Aunt Elaine would meet a tragic end as a teenager. In 1941, when my mother was 17 and in high school, she and Elaine were walking home in the early evening on the Fourth of July. With about a mile to go, the intense rays of the setting sun disoriented a driver, who veered off the road. The car missed my mother, but struck Elaine and killed her. My mom was devastated and ran home to get help, but it was already too late. My mother didn't talk much about this episode.

To provide income, my mother started working at a very young age, milking cows two times a day and working in the beet fields in Idaho. When I was old enough to understand, I wondered if her own childhood instability had put her on the path of seeking a religious foundation that could not be toppled by an economic or other force. It was her grandmother Rainey who taught her the Lord's Prayer, and Mom would later become an avid Bible reader.

My parents were both raised during the Great Depression in the thirties. Mom was frugal: she glued pink Pearl erasers to the underside of the toilet seat when the plastic tabs came off. I remember going to the bathroom to do a number-three (more on that later), and I would see pink Pearl erasers in the bowl. I thought I had a disease. (Let's just call it eraser disease.) She handed down underwear from my oldest brother to me and then on to my younger brother. The final stage of our community underwear was being bleached and used as dishrags until they disintegrated entirely. I'm not sure which I thought was more gross: sharing underwear, or drying clean dishes with underwear that had been worn by three boys. To this day I will not wear tighty-whities!

In 1944, after their high school graduations, my parents went to San Diego because Ben had joined the U.S. Navy. He shipped out, and on his first leave they had two days to get married. Their honeymoon was a night out drinking with a few of Dad's Navy buddies. Amid the revelry a fight broke out and, rather than protesting, my mother joined the melee and started hitting one of the opponents with her camera. Two days later Dad was out to sea again, to save the world from Nazis. I believe my mom stayed in San Diego for a while, so that she was there when her husband came back on leave each time the ship docked. She went to nursing school, but only briefly, because she passed out the first time she saw blood. She ended up working as an office assistant instead.

Dad never talked about the war, but the last half of 1944 was brutal in the Pacific theater where he'd gone. Among other jobs, he was a projectionist on the ship who ran the movies for the crew. He also saw heavy action, when Japanese kamikaze pilots terrorized their ship. He lost friends, was certain he was going to die, and for much of his life had nightmares about the commingled smell of burning oil and human flesh. I believe that experience was an accelerant that acted on the original seed of his anger toward his own father. It was easier to hate the U.S. military for subjecting him to such horror, than to somehow process and resolve his emotions. He eventually channeled that simmering rage toward his wife and his own children.

After the war my parents ended up in Spokane, Washington, where I was born November 9, 1947, at either Deaconess Hospital or Sacred Heart Hospital. I had curly light-brown hair. If it's possible, I actually seem to recall taking my first steps, near the stairs from the living room that led upstairs. I took my initial steps at the bottom of the stairs as someone held their hands out to me. It may have been my dad. I was the second child and second son in a family that would eventually include seven of us children. Only my older brother Lee and I were born in Spokane; the rest of my siblings would be born after we moved to Idaho around the time I turned 3 years old.

As a child I didn't understand how children were born: I just thought my mom had them automatically every two years, because new offspring arrived in our family like clockwork. My mom and dad had three boys in a row, and then four girls: Lee, me, Dean, Sue, Kay, Jo, and Marie. Mom was 48 when Marie was born. My youngest sister Marie is just three months older than my daughter Tiffany. I was close to my younger brother Dean. He and I spent a lot of time together, much of it getting into trouble—usually initiated by yours truly!

I never got along much with my older brother Lee. In the years Lee and I were raised together, I don't believe he spoke more than a hundred words to me. In some ways he was quiet and isolated from the rest of the family, like our dad. From my perspective, Lee harbored a lot of internal anger, which I suppose all us Bolen children did in different ways. Lee never showed his anger outwardly, but I could see he was tense. When conflicts arose, he would withdraw and walk away—except one time in junior high school he came to my defense during a fight. I remember he'd write "L.R. Bolen" on everything he owned. Lee really didn't have much emotional connection to any of us siblings.

Admittedly, because Lee reminded me of my dad (isolated and noncommunicative), I intentionally sought ways to irritate him. I once heard him playing music in his bedroom. When I swung open the door and saw him dancing, I started laughing. Immature, yes, but those are the ways I needled my older brother. Lee played basketball, but was never a starter like our superstar younger brother Dean. Instead, Lee spent all his time working at our dad's store. Looking back now, I have a lot of empathy for what Lee went through as the oldest child, with the burden of expectations, and never being as good at basketball as Dean, which carried a lot of weight with our father.

When Lee graduated from high school, his number came up in the draft for Vietnam; our parents were very upset. Lee joined the U.S. Army and was scheduled to go to Vietnam, but somehow Dad intervened via a U.S. senator, which kept Lee safely home. I'm grateful he did not have to go fight in what I believed was an unjust war. Lee only dated one girl, and is still married to Sarah more than fifty years later at this writing in 2021.

I remember my mom taking black-and-white eight-millimeter movies on a Bell and Howell film camera. In one film I'm in the snow hitting a basketball with a small hoe. Even at 3 I wanted to be in front of the camera, so I hit the ball all over the place to attract the filmmaker's gaze.

I don't remember a lot about my young childhood, but one thing I do remember is being dressed up as a girl. My mother, the filmmaker, caught that on film, too, and showed it to my family and relatives. I was 5 and horrified. I went to my room and cried. My younger brother Dean had also been unwittingly cast in this production, also playing the part of a boy dressed up as a girl.

Because there were so many of us kids to wrangle, Mom was always harried, with little time alone with any one child. She was able to offer more affection than our dad, but not by much. Part of that, I believe, was a generational thing; parents in the forties and fifties were your parents, not your friends. My mother was a great caretaker of our family, but was not very emotionally connected to us. Her job was to be strong, work hard, and move the family forward.

I did share one powerful way of bonding with my mom. She would sit on the couch and read her Bible. I'd lay my head in her lap. She would rub my hair with one of her hands while she read.

To this day I still love to have my head rubbed. Out of the three of us Bolen boys, my mother and I were the closest. I truly loved my mom, to the point I would insert myself between her and the wrath of my dad.

SINCE my dad didn't talk to me much, the paternal side of my family of origin is full of shadowy figures. My paternal grandparents lived in Meridian, Idaho. My grandfather Frank Bolen, too, rarely spoke to me. I remember him wearing bib overalls, sitting in a chair in front of the stove in the living room, and smoking cigarettes. My paternal grandmother Sallie was a devout Nazarene. By the time I was in high school she was practically crippled with severe rheumatoid arthritis. She'd shuffle around the house in a dress, an apron, and chunky black orthopedic shoes, which is the attire in which she'd always welcome us. Grandma had short, curly, salt-and-pepper hair and whiskers on her chin. She was always happy to see us when we came to visit her. When we visited, we'd been instructed to temper our hugs so as not to break her apart.

They lived caddy-corner from a small park that hosted auto races. If we were visiting on a Saturday night we got to see the track lights turn on, and we'd hear the announcer's voice crackle over the loudspeaker. Once the races were underway, the dust from the track would waft across the street. That track is still there to this day; it's paved now, but I can remember the smell of that dust lingering around their house on a summer Saturday night. Their small house was made of large stones, with a huge tree in the front yard that was struck by lightning when we were there. It sounded like an explosion and split the tree to the ground. Somehow that tree survived and marked the milestones of my childhood, as I'd come to visit and watch it get bigger and bigger over the years. The back of the house had a cellar we would venture into, which was dark, full of spiders, and downright creepy. Grandma had a garden that she wasn't able to tend once she got sick. I remember her cooking for us, in her small kitchen, even when she had arthritis. Grandpa never budged, just sat in his chair and smoked. Before she got sick, my grandma used to work as a cook, and occasionally filled in as a waitress, at Pat's Café in Meridian. Toward the end, Grandma Sallie was so skinny and frail that when she dropped a broom on her leg it tore her skin all the way down from her knee to the ankle. They took her to the doctor, who tried to stitch her up but her skin was so rotten it didn't take. She died after our family had moved away to Alaska.

BACK to my mom's side of the family; everybody, including me, loved Grandma Vera. She was the main adult relative from my formative years who I can recall entirely, knew well, and genuinely liked. She was a kind and loving person. She was an early, and perhaps my only, adult advocate in my younger years. Whenever I went to her house she said, "You gotta eat something... let's see what I have." And then she would put on a four-course dinner even if I had already eaten. She insisted we eat, so each time I left her house as fat as a tick.

When I was in my late twenties, Grandma Vera accurately predicted something no one could have known for the future Sears Roebuck and Company men's clothing salesman.

"I have this feeling you're going to be a millionaire by the time you're 30," she said.

With that, she planted possibilities in me in ways I'd never get at home where I was afraid and voiceless. And in the religion my mother would soon immerse herself, no one would ever talk about financial success because it was considered worldly. But here was Grandma Vera, giving me permission to be important, make a difference, and succeed in big ways.

Grandma Vera made something called "lumpy dick," a flour, milk, and cinnamon concoction that no one could say with a straight face and that actually tasted much better than it sounded. She served it to her kids during the Great Depression. *The world is in a devastating economic slump and downward spiral: Eat your lumpy dick!*

She loved to watch car racing, and we would take her to the same Meridian Speedway caddy-corner to my paternal grandparents' house. She told me she was always hoping for a good crash (as long as no one got hurt). She and I had a blast doing that together and laughing when the cars collided. She and Grandpa Orvid had the same Boise State men's basketball season tickets for almost fifty years. They eventually had to stop attending as their health waned, and during the last game they would ever attend, the Boise State staff gave them a beautiful blanket and a special award announced over the loudspeakers, which saluted Vera and Orvid as the most dedicated fans ever.

Grandma Vera lived a grand life, and almost made it to 100 years old—she died at age 99. Services and the viewing were at a Mormon church in Boise, during which I slipped a note in her casket. In the note I told her how much I loved her and how important she was in my life. To me she was a perfect grandmother, the single greatest nurturing presence of my youth and early adulthood. Long before she died, she said something I never forgot: "Danny, I just want you to always be you. Never give up being you."

More prescient words were never spoken to me, prior or since. But it was going to take me many decades to finally embrace Grandma Vera's full wisdom.

Four

How Soon Can You Get On a Plane?

FORTY-FIVE YEARS BEFORE I TOOK THE FLIGHT to Cleveland to get my heart assessed, I took my first flight to Cleveland for a job interview with Management Recruiters. After dazzling the bouffant twins at Snelling and Snelling, I had moved on to another executive search firm called Dunhill, which operated based more on employer-paid fees. That meant when I placed someone, the hiring company paid us, which also meant I wouldn't have to chase down my own candidates for payments.

At Dunhill, the S&S smoking tandem was replaced by the non-smoking Keith Kirkpatrick, an executive so conservative he made Richard Nixon look like a pot-smoking hippie. Dunhill was smaller than Snelling and Snelling, and still exists to this day. But from the outset, Mr. Kirkpatrick was not in the class of the bouffant twins. My performance was never the issue: In just two years I had single-handedly tripled his total volume. He rewarded me by cutting my commissions. I rewarded him by giving him my two weeks' notice, which was received remarkably similarly to my resignation from Sears.

"That's your choice," he said. "But don't bother sticking around. Just leave the key under the door." From that experience I learned a tenet: Never cut your top producer's commissions. Ever. I would never accept such a cut myself or foist one on my own employees. True to my work ethic, I stayed until 9 p.m. on my last day at the office while he was on his way to Mexico for a vacation. I slipped my office key under the door and was done with Dunhill—although Mr. Kirkpatrick still owed me $8,000 in commissions, which he never paid.

"I never want to see or talk to you again," I said the last time I ever spoke to him. "You're stealing from me." Two years later I saw Keith Kirkpatrick on an airplane; he wouldn't even look at me.

"This is Dan Bolen," I said over the phone in 1976, again deploying my direct approach to getting hired at another new company, Management Recruiters. They had been my top competitor, which is why I respected them and wanted to work there.

"I'd like to open a franchise," I said. I was talking to Bob Anderson, director of franchises for Management Recruiters, who was at his office on Euclid Avenue in Cleveland. Bob Anderson had never met or heard of me until this first phone call, which came out of the blue for him but was something I had long planned as an escape from the anchor Keith Kirkpatrick had secured around my neck.

"Where?" Bob Anderson asked.

"Boise, Idaho."

"Iowa?"

"Idaho."

"We're not interested in Idaho," he said. "It won't work."

"I disagree," I said.

Pause. Salespeople hiring salespeople often admired such immediate redirects. "What were your billings at... where did you say you worked?"

"Dunhill."

"That's right. How much?"

"More than $200,000 a year in total billings."

Another pause, longer than the first. It turns out Bob Anderson, too, could be direct: "How soon can you get on a plane?"

Be careful what you ask for: I went to Cleveland and got the gig. Regional manager Bob Maxwell came to Boise to help me set up my new operation. Eventually Bob would come to consider me the best recruiter in the United States. To tout my talents, he wrote an article about me entitled "The Robo Recruiter" for the main industry publication, called *The Fordyce Letter*. He used a pseudonym so I wouldn't be inundated with calls from recruiters around the country looking for the magic formula to success. (Here's a helpful hint: Find your passion, whether it's corporate recruiting or candlemaking. You can only be truly successful when you find your passion, which will propel you through the tough times.)

Before all that, I was 27 and had $8,000 in our savings account. I had to come up with $100,000 for the franchise fee, which meant borrowing $92,000, unsecured. No bank was going to touch that big of a non-collateralized note with an unproven kid in his twenties, so that left me with one dreadful option.

Going back to my father.

Yes, that father.

Hat in hand.

THE big family secret in our house growing up (well, at least *one* of the big secrets) was Dad's emotional and physical abuse of everyone in the household. That's why we weren't allowed to ever have a friend sleep over. Our father was a powder keg who could explode almost without warning. Dad was never really connected emotionally to either my mom or any of his own children. He himself was raised with the idea that a father's job was to support the family financially—and, well, that's where the responsibility ended. So he was either working to support us, or spending any free time drinking. Our mother kowtowed to him. She would prepare his drinks and serve him his food at his TV tray while we ate in the kitchen, to keep the powder away from the ignition sources.

Whenever he finished his drink, he would just silently raise his cup. Mom would swoop in with a quick refill, which bugged me. Dad always ended his meal with vanilla ice cream made at Albertsons, where he was a store manager for more than twenty years. There were not fights every night, but several times a week we'd hear the commotion from our beds. We would hear loud arguing, rage, things being toppled, and then a disconcerting quietness, which I believe was when he was physically abusing her. I don't believe my mother ever physically fought back, but she would yell. After these big blowouts it was common for Dad not to speak to the family for a week or two, a full month, and sometimes even longer. He'd actually clam up and not speak a word to his wife, or any of his seven children, for weeks straight. I'm not sure how he did it.

There was always a fear for us kids and Mom alike that any utterance might prompt Dad to berate, belittle, or physically abuse us. There were times, too, when my mother used some physical force to correct one of her three sons. But her hand slaps and spankings were like a visit to the ice cream truck compared to Dad's wrath.

However, there was one time I remember, when I was 16 and likely said something asinine to my mom. She hit me across the face with a broom handle and said she was going to tell Dad when he got home, which she did. My dad grabbed me by the arm and came down with a fist with so much force it lifted me off the ground. And not just once: he would go on and on, over and over again, until I collapsed. It seemed like the more he unleashed his violence the more it fed his rage, rather than relieving it. He would give me this black-eyed look as he bit his tongue, like a shark chomping in bloody waters. I don't believe he knew how hard he was hitting us. I still have bad memories about those assaults as he bit his tongue. My brothers Lee and Dean took their share, but of the seven of us Bolen children, I was the most emotional and the only one who would stand up to my father when we saw him hit my mother. I would scream at him, *You're not going to do that to her!* That would get his attention, like poking a feeding bear, and he would redirect his predatory gaze, clenched tongue, and violence toward me by beating me.

Lee was quite introverted and didn't challenge Dad. Dean was his favorite because he was so good at basketball. My sister Sue would plead with me not to challenge Dad, but I couldn't stand to let him go unchecked. The police were never involved; this was our original family secret. We were all afraid to seek outside help, to even tell anyone, because we had to appear to be the family that had it all together. I never spoke about the abuse outside our home, and I don't believe any of my brothers or sisters did, either.

I eventually came to understand that my Dad's way of dealing with my emotions was to beat them out of me. For that, I learned to hate him. He never gave me a single compliment in my entire life. Dad had so much anger; my mother and all seven of us Bolen children tried to walk the line that would keep him from exploding.

I took all that anger directed at me and channeled it toward being a people pleaser: *If I can keep you happy, then you won't hurt me.* Of course, I didn't understand that's what I was doing, nor could I articulate it, but that's who I became. I became a rule follower, too, as part of the formula to survive. It didn't matter that the rule book we'd been handed was completely illogical, insane, and inhumane. Those were the rules you followed to avoid terror, trauma, and physical pain. Dad's rage fueled my competitive drive to be the best—because, just maybe, if I was the best at something then he would accept me as his son and stop distancing himself from me and hitting me when his anger was out of control. Even after he was long dead, his rage continued to fuel me into the financial stratosphere.

Nonetheless, I went to him and asked for money. "I want to open my own franchise," I told Dad. "And I need a loan."

"You know I'm going to have to charge you interest."

Since I was 27, he no longer had the power to lord over me physically. Instead, he wielded whatever power he could by holding emotional sway. He agreed to the loan, but told me I had to turn around and walk backward toward him, palms up, to accept the $92,000 check he'd written (with interest to be added to the payback amount). Even as I approached 30 I was still a rule follower. My father wanted to make me grovel, so I groveled. I followed his rules because following rules equaled survival, and to survive I had to get the loan. It would take me most of my life to figure out that this overly zealous rigidity to following rules was a trait that made me especially vulnerable to the sort of brainwashing used in cults to control group members.

All this, and he still didn't know the really big secret. I'd taken one of the family rules for self preservation *(Don't tell anyone what's really happening at home)* and applied it to myself as a shield of protective deceit *(Don't be yourself because it's not safe)*. And my shield was so thick no one knew my secret. Not even me, really, because I was a good family man, married, with a daughter, and killing it in my career. Just ask Lynn Haynes or Keith Kirkpatrick.

When I paid my father back completely in a few months, including the interest, he had the gall to ask: "Do you want to borrow more?"

I wasn't worthy of his love or a hug. Or unconditional regard, or at least not being physically beaten. But I was a good money bet, like a well-muscled racehorse. I wanted to cry, but that sadness immediately crystallized into anger. Screw you!

That thought was immediately voided by *The Family Rule Book*, which clearly specified the correct response.

"No, thank you," I said. "I'm good."

Five

Paradise Lost

IN THE LATE FIFTIES, MY MOM UNDERWENT A secret baptism in Blackfoot, Idaho. To do so, she had to leave us three boys ice skating on a frozen pond on a bitter, hazy day I remember as mind-numbingly cold. The three of us wondered where she had gone, and whether she had somehow forgotten us, and left us to fend for ourselves.

The march toward that odd day had started a decade earlier, in 1947, when we were still living in Spokane, Washington, where I had been born. There was a knock on the door, and a man and a woman told Mom they were Jehovah's Witnesses. Mom had been raised as a Mormon, in Utah, by her mother. This couple quietly explained that there were contradictions between the Book of Mormon and the Bible, which Mom vehemently denied.

Because she was a seeker herself, rather than sending the unsolicited visitors on their way and forgetting the entire matter, Mom undertook her own personal investigation, for *the next three years*, studying and comparing the Book of Mormon to the American Standard Bible. And, alas, she came to the same conclusion: that there were indeed contradictions she could no longer deny or overcome with her previous logic and reasoning.

In 1950, my mother started studying the Bible with a lady in the local congregation of Jehovah's Witnesses, and this sent her down a new path. However, switching religions was just the sort of thing that might ignite her husband's rage, on sheer principle, so the six of us children (the youngest was not yet born) were unwittingly pulled into the ruse. Caught in the middle with no say in the matter, we now had another family secret to guard: Mom's religion.

When Dad was at work, which was most of the time, Mom unfurled her secret teaching materials and went to work to enlighten us. She had an orange book called *Paradise Lost, Paradise Regained* that she read aloud to us. I was a very young child when these covert spiritual operations began, and didn't absorb much of it. I remember several times when Dad would unexpectedly come home for lunch, and we had to shove the Bibles and literature under the couch to hide the illicit contraband. Even before I understood what my mom was attempting to impart, I sensed this religion was creating problems in my life and in my family. And so, I began to resist it.

On most days, Mom stowed the Jehovah's Witness materials safely and fed us dinner at the kitchen table by the time Dad got home. He would then sit by himself at the TV tray in the living room, where Mom served him dinner and a highball. After dinner he'd continue watching TV and drinking highballs until he fell asleep. To my memory, we rarely had a family meal together. Even if he was passed out and snoring, we were not allowed to change the channel, even when the screen had gone to static fuzz, because if awakened he'd yell, "I'm watching this!"

Rule 96: Don't touch the television controls!

When I was around 6 years old, we moved to a house on ten acres just off Bott Lane. It was a small house with a detached garage that had dirt floors. I remember Dad used to throw his cigarette butts onto the dirt; I would later retrieve them and smoke the butts down to the filters. We had a few cows and a chicken coop. There were stacked bales of hay and a huge gasoline container. I would climb up on that container, unscrew the cap, and smell the gas. I loved the smell of gasoline. One time I sniffed so many fumes the leaves from the nearby oak tree seemed to whirl as I fell off the container.

One year I got a BB gun for Christmas. Later, on a cold, snowy day, I tramped around outside for an hour trying to find a bird, and ended up on the roof of the detached garage. Since there were no birds to be found, when my older brother Lee came out of the house I figured he was as good a target as any and shot him in the back of the head. He was enraged. He chased me to the top of the hay bales, and then I fell through the chicken coop. This elicited a severe beating from Dad, one that left bruises that turned all sorts of lurid colors. I'd broken the first and most basic rule.

Rule 1: Don't piss off Dad.

In 1952, for first grade at Locust Elementary School, my teacher was Mrs. McPherson. The next year I had Mrs. Vargas, who was my favorite teacher because she always talked about the little blue elf during story time. She told us the little blue elf would visit each of our houses, and she always made it a fascinating and believable tale. The little blue elf, in fact, once snuck into our house and hid in the dryer. That meant, I surmised, that the little blue elf was in on our secret religious teachings, too—and I wished I could ask him what he thought of Mom's overall thesis as the basis to switch from one team of Christians to another, from Team Mormon to Team JW. And, I reasoned, if the little blue elf knew one secret, he surely knew them all. That was a comforting thought, and I was grateful I had the little blue elf to shoulder some of the burden of hiding so many secrets and remembering all the rules.

When we needed to use the toilet in Mrs. Vargas' class, we had to hold up our fingers: one meant pee, two meant poo. When I raised three fingers Mrs. Vargas asked what that meant. Easy: I had to do both. As with everything else in my life, I was an overachiever in my classes. I pretty much made straight A's, not because I was the smartest but because I worked hard, which kept me distracted from the challenges in my household and the secrets we all harbored. My third-grade teacher was Mrs. Chenowith, who was the oldest of the three teachers I'd had; she had gray hair in a bun. She would play baseball with us during recess. She even played catcher and crouched down like Joe Garagiola, except she was in her dress and black granny shoes behind home plate.

At home, somehow we kept Dad in the dark long enough for me to absorb most of the basic tenets of Mom's newfound belief system. I didn't make this connection at the time, between our well-established family structure and Mom's new religion, but as a Jehovah's Witness, she taught us that there were rules to follow, and then more rules, and yet more rules after that. We would worship the one true and almighty God, whose name was Jehovah. That made sense: They named the religion after the Creator. The followers of the religion were witnesses to all the great things He offered, now and for eternity. And they would witness to others in the community about Jehovah and His purpose for the earth; this was their preaching and teaching activity to the community before the end would come at Armageddon.

She told us we'd follow the Bible, all sixty-six books, including both testaments. And JWs, she said, followed the Bible literally, except the few parts that teach symbolically. Again, not a bad approach as far as Bible interpretations go. As far as Jesus, He was only the son of God, not the Almighty, so basically the

Catholics had it all wrong because there's no scriptural basis for the trinity doctrine. To achieve salvation—i.e., to escape sin and death—one had to exercise faith in Jesus, learn the truth about Jehovah God, preach and teach the good news to others, and get baptized. Phew, talk about a long list of rules with dozens of sub-rules beneath each of those! It was a requirement that you had to share in the preaching activity in the door-to-door ministry before you were allowed to be baptized. Your baptism day would be the date you became an ordained minister, and then you were held accountable for all your actions. Mom would be the first among us to take that final step, in secret, while we were ice skating.

The JW entrance requirements for Heaven were a little murky to the young me, because apparently only 144,000 will qualify. I always wondered: Why that number, and not fewer or a whole lot more on a planet with billions of people? They base it on two Bible verses, in Revelation 7 and 14, that discuss 144,000 people from *"...every tribe of the sons of Israel."* To get into that exclusive group, Jehovah Himself can call you as one of the 144,000.

Those who are called simply *know* they've been called, which is what my mom believed: She had been called by God to ascend to Heaven. (By the way, at the time of this writing there were still about 8,000 slots remaining—although the number keeps increasing, which always puzzled me.) Meanwhile, for all the other obedient people, Earth will be the eternal home, a paradise of perfect health and perfect life.

The JWs were pretty clear on Satan: All evil and suffering began when this fallen angel coaxed the first human couple, Adam and Eve, to join him in rebellion, and they brought pain and death to all their offspring. As a child, one aspect I remember liking was the absence of a fiery Hell. For JWs, Hell is the grave; there is no hellfire. Instead, for JWs, all the billions who have died and passed out of existence will get a second chance at resurrection courtesy of Jehovah. But it will be a limited one-time offer: Those who refuse to adopt His ways will then be left in the grave (Hell) and not resurrected. But, again, just gone and at least not relegated to hellfire.

One aspect I've always liked is that Jehovah's Witnesses are peaceful and will not participate in warfare. However, they also profess unselfish love and avoid practices that displease God, which includes rejecting blood transfusions. Even as a youth, I never understood why saving a life would displease God, but who was I to question Jehovah? Instead, we were being instructed to follow the rules laid out before us.

One of my favorite scriptures, which I continue to believe and attempt to live by to this day, is from Galatians 5:22 and 5:23: *"On the other hand, the fruitage of the spirit is love, joy, peace, patience, kindness, goodness, faith, mildness, and self-control."* Religion aside, if we all aspired to live by these nine principles the world would be a much better place for everyone.

The church was organized into congregations that were each managed by a group of elders. How unfathomable it would have seemed to me at the time to be told I would one day be one of those elders. At church, they never passed the basket. Instead, members were supposed to just put cash or checks in the contribution boxes at the back of the Kingdom Hall. This was another aspect I admired, because the collections were anonymous, which freed people from being shamed for not giving enough, or admired for giving a lot. Oh yeah, that was another thing we learned: The places of worship were called Kingdom Halls, not churches (in this memoir we use "Kingdom Hall" and "church" interchangeably).

Jehovah's Witnesses, Mom told us, were not big on symbols, images, and venerating the cross; they were doers. Get baptized. Pray to God. Read, study and meditate on the Bible. Attend five meetings a week at the Kingdom Hall, which included three evenings. Go knock on doors, preach, and teach the good news of the kingdom. Follow the rules. My mom shared stories of meeting some of the bravest people—Jehovah's Witnesses who were terrified of public speaking, door-knocking, and talking to strangers—who pushed that fear aside to honor their deep-seated faith and beliefs. (As an adult I would become one of those door-knockers, but we'll get to that later.)

"Love your neighbor as yourself" seemed reasonable to me, as did defining marriage as the union of one man and one woman—because that's all I knew: Mom and Dad. What other option was there? One tenet would come back to haunt me: that sexual immorality was the only valid basis for a scriptural divorce. But as a boy, the adult stuff of marriage and divorce were clearly just faraway and vague concepts, not actual things that pertained to me in any way.

Of course, eventually Dad figured out what was going on with Mom's secret teachings—and, predictably, he blew his stack. *Rule 1: Don't piss off Dad.* Mom had been continually instilling into our heads that we had to prepare for Armageddon, that it would soon be upon us. When she and Dad fought about her new religion and how she had been teaching us in secret, we all believed their loud explosions of anger were Armageddon's opening act. Then the fights got worse when Mom's undercover proselytizing evolved into openly going door-to-door to spread the JW word, which is how she had discovered "the truth," as the JW liked to call their version of religion.

This was a bridge too far for Dad, who was angered and completely embarrassed when neighbors would recognize Mom as the wife of the manager of the Albertsons grocery store. Founder Joe Albertson always espoused giving first-class service to each customer, including never making a customer wait. My dad embraced that creed like his own religion. Therefore, to have his wife going door-to-door foisting her beliefs on people was just too much, a clear sin and violation of his customer-service dogma.

At the time, Dad believed JWs were dullards, people to be avoided. True to the toxicity and crazymaking in our family, decades later my dad became a JW himself, and went into full-time ministry for more than twenty years. He, too, was a big fan of a thick new rule book to follow alongside our own family volume. And hearing that news would stun me: I would have believed Satan would find and embrace the truth before my father ever would.

Despite Mom's best attempts, by the time I was a teenager and then headed off to college I was mostly agnostic. And it's not like I didn't understand the religious material, because my mom had taught it to us. On a daily basis, JWs read and study the Bible. To that end, much later in my life, I would read the entire Bible eighteen times in eighteen years—from Genesis, "In the beginning God created the heavens and the earth…" through Revelation, "May the undeserved kindness of the Lord Jesus be with the holy ones."

Despite my relatively solid grip on the subject matter, whether there was or wasn't a God just wasn't a top-line priority for me. I held onto the few parts I liked, such as not having any belief in hellfire: when you died you went to the grave to wait. Then it would be up to God to resurrect you to life on Earth (assuming you were redeemable). That appealed to me. I also liked the stance of being peaceful and opposing war, the most heinous barbarism in human history. How could I ever kill another human being, whether sanctioned by the U.S. government or not?

I liked most of what our mom taught us, but I also connected the practice of being a Jehovah's Witness—or following any religion, for that matter—with pain, for what it had wrought in my own family. Religion was another toxic secret within a family of toxic secrets. And another long set of ridiculous rules I didn't need.

Secrets and ridiculous family rules: I already had enough of those to lug around.

Six

When You're Off the Phone, You're Unemployed

WITH THE LOAN FROM MY DAD, IN 1976 MY recruiting operation was in business with three franchises under one roof: Management Recruiters, Sales Consultants (handled solely by me), and Office Mates 5 (run by women to place office staff). Our office was on Shoreline next to the Boise River. We had one big room filled with five desks and a conference room. My space was among the desks in the back corner. In the winter the office was cold, and in the summer hot and stuffy, because the building systems never worked very well. Although the building was on the banks of the Boise River, the series of large windows faced the other way toward the parking lot. While much more scenic, the riverfront spaces were more expensive, so I opted for the uninspired view of the parking lot.

Using the money from my dad, I'd signed the lease, paid the initial rent, and modestly furnished the office with Hon desks, which were metal with laminated wood tops. They were cheap and serviceable, like the matching Hon chairs, which were metal framed with vinyl cushions. The office didn't have to impress anyone; our mission would be primarily carried out by being on the telephone. Any applicants or employers who did come by the office wouldn't be there long, so no need to spend lavishly on decorator touches.

Our strategy would differ from the two previous firms where I'd cut my teeth. We would operate using a two-tiered system of both employer- and applicant-paid fees. We focused locally for candidates and employers in and around Boise, and then branched out to regional and national employers and candidates. Effectively recruiting was always a delicate balance, because we were serving two masters: employers (sources) and candidates. The company that loved you one day for finding a stellar employee might hate you the next if you pilfered another employee to go work elsewhere. I always honored the approach that if I placed a candidate with a company that was a client, I would not take their people, because I believed it was morally wrong. That was how I operated for my entire career, and the philosophy I taught those in my employ. I started with a team of just six people including myself.

Our receptionist, Kim Waxelman, sat up front with her IBM Selectric typewriter always in motion. I later hired my younger brother, Dean, who recruited in the insurance field, finding underwriters and adjusters for large companies such as Safeco and Maryland Casualty. Gene Schwartz targeted accounting, and Doug Malone focused on technical engineering positions. Cindy Mann, a take-charge and no-nonsense woman like a bulldozer in a dress, and Belinda Bennett ran Office Mates 5, focusing on administrative positions—almost entirely for women during the late seventies. Heading up Sales Consultants was yours truly: I focused on marketing and sales positions in both consumer and industrial concerns, including Procter & Gamble and Norwich, among dozens and dozens of other companies.

We started each work day with a brief morning meeting; again, no one was making money unless we were on the telephone. I set out the schedule I followed and expected everyone else to follow, too. From 8 to 8:30 a.m. it was time to organize the day's strategy. Then the real work began, for three hours from 8:30 to 11:30 a.m.: marketing calls, or SOD calls as we called them at Snelling and Snelling. My unique strategy was to use the marketing calls to tout our top-rated candidates to employers who weren't even advertising an open position.

Spin of the dial!

For decades, my work life revolved around making telephone calls, through each leap in technology: rotary dial, push button, and cellular. Like bricklayers with a daily quota, we each had to make a minimum of fifty calls each day. And we couldn't just leave fifty messages: regardless of how many calls it took, we each had to speak to at least ten actual clients every day. We always started with our MPCs, our most placeable candidates. Through it all I was part taskmaster and part cheerleader, throwing out Zig Ziglar gems from the sideline like a coach with a flat-top buzz cut:

—*Make enough calls to celebrate the "no."*

—*A "no" can become a "yes."*

—*When something bad happens, there's always a gift you can't yet see.*

—*You have to move a lot of dirt to find the treasure.*

—*We'll be the last business that takes down our sign.* (During recessions, we just doubled our call volume).

—*When you're off the phone, you're unemployed.*

—*Never take your employers and candidates for granted.*

—*You have the power to choose the color of the grandchild's eyes.*

Wait, what!? That last one was always a show-stopper, a Dan Bolen original. As one example of many, I placed a husband and wife who lived in Houston in new positions in New Orleans, where they eventually had a child. That child later attended Louisiana State University in Baton Rouge, where she met her future husband, got married, and had a child. Our work, I posited, potentially had a wide influence on people's lives—including the color of their grandchildren's eyes.

At work, I never stopped moving. Cindy Mann and Belinda Bennett never stopped smoking, because no one knew about second-hand smoke during the Jimmy Carter administration. When I wasn't on the phone making my own calls, I was circulating around the office and keeping tabs on everyone. After the initial morning blitz we all paused for half an hour to organize again, from 11:30 a.m. to noon, before breaking for a one-hour lunch. During the summer, Belinda Bennett would disappear during the lunch break. When she returned, she was always sweaty. After weeks of this, I finally had to ask.

"Belinda, why are you always sweaty after lunch?"

"I go sunbathe by the river."

"In your dress?"

She laughed. "No, I change into my bikini and lie on the grass."

I wasn't quite sure what to say. The next day, during lunch hour I went out to see for myself and, sure enough, Belinda was sprawled out on her towel in her pink bikini, displaying her knockout body. When I turned and looked back at the building with the more expensive riverfront offices, I could see a row of men taking in the view. I decided that was her way of marketing herself to potential suitors.

After the lunch break we organized again to prepare for our recruiting calls, from 1 to 1:30 p.m. Then we stormed the beaches at Normandy again from 1:30 to 4:30 p.m. to do our recruiting calls. There were two parts of the business: after our morning marketing calls, we used the afternoon to take our most marketable job openings and find candidates to fill those positions. Those recruiting calls were initiated by job orders (which we'd secured by marketing, or they came in unsolicited) to find candidates from competitor companies.

We followed all that with a final hour, from 4:30 to 5:30 p.m., to organize one more time and complete paperwork. We used the total of two hours of down time each day to also debrief employers and candidates on interviews and pull more candidates from our files for new job order positions we'd received, in addition to handling job offers being made to our candidates. In truth, no one ever left much before 6:30 p.m. And I would tell anyone who left on the button, at 5:30 p.m., that they were never going to be successful. I ran a tight ship, and it made people successful. We each kept our top candidate interviews on a hot sheet, which I reviewed daily. I was courteous and direct: "Why has this candidate been on your hot sheet for two days with no more interviews scheduled?"

There was constant pressure to keep the revolving doors spinning: candidates and job orders found, candidates interviewed, candidates placed. This was not a daily routine for the timid, unmotivated, or weak-willed. Anyone who didn't like, or couldn't keep pace with, the regimented approach and steady workload quickly dropped off and went elsewhere to find a more suitable line of work. Those of us who stayed were phone warriors who could not be dissuaded from the mission by any force on the other end of the telephone. This was the era before headsets, which meant holding the receiver for hours and being anchored to the desk. We loved the action, thrived, and made a lot of money. Cindy and Belinda each burned through a half a pack or more of cigarettes every day while on the phones. My brother Dean was a natural and followed everything I suggested. Gene Schwartz, Doug Malone, my brother, and I all wore shirts and ties—required, because I told them when you dressed professionally you spoke professionally. I never asked any of my employees to do something I wasn't doing myself. I was right there in the trenches with them, knee-deep in the mud, every step of the way. That passion for being in the midst of the action, I later realized, fueled my work addiction.

The first year I personally made more than $100,000 in income, which was a lot for a 28-year-old who'd just struck out on his own. The next year I doubled my income. Everyone was doing well. During our third year, we switched to employer-paid fees only, because it was just cleaner and simpler to tap the business rather than the applicant. We were the first recruiting company in Idaho to switch to employer-paid fees. On May 1 that year we published an advertisement in the Idaho Statesman: *Mayday! Mayday! Management Recruiters of Boise have gone one hundred percent employer retained fees!* Many people thought we were crazy, but I was used to doing crazy; coming from the Bolen household, crazy was comfortable. It wouldn't take long until we became the number-one Management Recruiters firm in the United States. Our business was populated with colorful characters.

One of the candidates we placed was a regional manager for Norwich Pharmaceutical Company, which made Pepto-Bismol, aspirin, and a birth control pill inserted vaginally with a plastic applicator. The pills came in square packages covered with tinfoil, so the user could pop out an individual pill. The manager we knew once received a letter from a woman who asked if the company could round the edges of the tinfoil because the package was painful to put in! However, she also commented that somehow the product worked very well.

We had another employer we nicknamed "Blue Boots," because he wore blue cowboy boots and always requested that we send only attractive women to interviews. When I told him we couldn't discriminate based on gender, and that we would continue to send male and female candidates, we learned the truth: He was actually just looking to put the moves on our candidates, not seriously consider them for open positions. We had to get rid of Blue Boots.

My brother Dean had the best candidate story of them all. He had recruited a property casualty underwriter, a well-qualified man who was very good-looking, in great shape, and always dressed to the nines. With his bachelor's degree and several years of insurance industry experience, he was a dream candidate. Dean presented him for a position and, as we suspected, our candidate did extremely well on the phone interview. Based on that, the company paid for him to travel to the regional headquarters in Los Angeles for a face-to-face interview. As the story goes, when he arrived at the building he looked like a male model. A spark of recognition lit up in the receptionist.

"I know you from somewhere," she said.

The stunning candidate just smiled.

"Yeah," she said. "I know I know you. I just don't know where…"

"Small world, right?" he said.

She dialed for her boss and let him know the candidate was there to interview. She couldn't resist a quick glance at his nice backside as he walked down the hall. Five minutes later, while she was typing a memo, it hit her: Mr. Candidate was that month's centerfold in *Playgirl* magazine! She started laughing hysterically. After the interview concluded and he'd left, she jokingly told her boss, "He papered himself all over the industry."

In the recruiting world, when a candidate "papered themselves all over the industry" it meant they'd indiscriminately sent résumés anywhere and everywhere. The boss got the joke, that Mr. Candidate had papered himself in a new and unique way, with his nude spread. They called my brother Dean and told him what had happened; as they were laughing hysterically, he and I decided there was only one final step in this unique placement process. We went together to the nearest convenience-store magazine rack and found the issue in question. Inside the store, Dean pushed the magazine on me and, of course, I feigned disgust at the prospect of opening it and deflected like a pro.

"Your candidate," I said, pushing the magazine back to him. "You look."

Dean looked, let out a gasp, nodded, and tossed the magazine back at me. "Oh my God, it's him!" There he was, the complete centerfold across both pages. That was my opportunity to look too, and sure enough, there was our very own Mr. Candidate, displaying another quite sizable attribute beyond those we already knew about.

OVER the course of my entire career, from 1969 at Snelling and Snelling to 2018 when I was in the last year of helming Dan Bolen and Associates, I survived eight recessions. By 1985 Ronald Reagan had replaced Jimmy Carter in the White House. I was the number-one performer, with the highest per-desk average of placements, among more than 600 Management Recruiters offices. Executives were calling and asking me to do seminars, to show others the magic formula to our success. And I was happy to abide, raking in hefty fees at a long run of sales conferences around the country and even internationally. I produced a seminar entitled *The Million Dollar Biller*, which I delivered coast-to-coast to Management Recruiter organizations and other executive search companies. I also produced videos of this seminar and other topics for Management Recruiters at the corporate office. Managers trained their staff with my videos, both at Management Recruiter offices and at executive search firms that had hired me to do seminars.

Was there a recipe I could share so that others could repeat our success? Well, yes and no. Anyone could buy the sheet music and lyrics to a Barbra Streisand song, sing it, and never sound like Barbra in a thousand years. So maybe I was the Barbra Streisand of the people business, which is how I've always viewed management recruiting. I've always had a passion for people and for life. And, unfortunately, most people didn't want to hear my real secret (well, not that secret, at least not yet). I truly believed, and still do, that when you find your real passion you'll become successful, because you'll never give up and therefore you'll succeed!

When I got my first fall-off at Management Recruiters—when a candidate you've placed doesn't work out—I was physically nauseated. After I got the call, I retreated to the nearest toilet, thinking I was about to throw up. And if this job was my passion, then I'd vomit with passion, too.

In reality, I could tell anyone the simple truth in three seconds over the phone, without flying across the country to deliver a seminar: I flat-out worked my ass off. At the expense of my marriage to Eileen, my relationship with my daughter, and even my relationship with myself. Everything I did was in service to the big two: helping my employers and candidates succeed, and religion.

Yes, the religion I was lukewarm about as I left home and went off to college in the sixties ruled my life by the mid-eighties (we're getting to that). Jehovah's Witnesses and my work both served a deeper purpose, which was to keep me from ever pausing long enough to face my own truth. Many years later I saw a quotation that summed it up perfectly: *The tragedy of life is not death, but what we let die inside of us while we live.*

Seven

I Understand. I Can See the Pain.

"I'M NOT INTERESTED," I TOLD BRUCE BENSON. "My mom's one of those."

And by that I meant she was JW, a Jehovah's Witness, just like Bruce had said he was. In fact, I later figured out that my mother had dispatched Bruce Benson to my dorm to lead me to "the truth." It was 1966, and I had finally reached critical velocity to escape my family, by coming here to the University of Alaska in Fairbanks, which was twelve hours north from Anchorage by train. I had acclimated to the cold, too, because in Fairbanks I was living just a couple hundred miles south of the Arctic Circle. That meant it had to hit ridiculous temperatures, maybe seventy-five below zero, for the weather to ever enter daily conversation. Otherwise you just bundled up and went about your business. In fact, anyone with a car had to plug in a head-bolt heater every night that kept the engine from freezing. When they would wake up in the morning and start the car, they would drive down the highway with all four tires feeling like they were flat until the air warmed up inside the tires; only then would they run smoothly.

More importantly, I had finally found a new sense of peace by getting away from my family, from the heavy religious dogma, the mental, physical, and emotional abuse from my dad, and the misplaced loyalty of a mother who had done little to protect her children from the wrath of the father.

Yes, I was finally free, ensconced in Lathrop Dormitory. I was the first in my family to go to college, where I would major in speech and drama. A man of letters, risen from the firestorm that might have portended a much darker turn in myself. And yet, despite all that, I also felt faint twinges of guilt and a sense of loss, because I was leaving behind the only family I thought I would ever have. Although my hatred of my father was well-justified by the overwhelming and damning evidence, that disdain also brought shame. He was, after all, still my dad. So when high school senior Bruce Benson knocked on my dorm room door and offered copies of *Watchtower* and *Awake* magazines, let's just say his JW gospel approach was not well received.

"Can I ask why?" he said.

Here we go... he sounded exactly like my mother had when she took me along a few times for door-knocking to spread "the truth."

"It's really personal for me," I said. I stiffened my arm across the door jamb to ensure Bruce Benson got the hint: He was not welcome here. He smiled and nodded.

"I understand how you feel," he said. "I know a lot of people, including myself, felt the same thing before discovering 'the truth.' And what we've all found is a way of life beyond anything we might have imagined." As a young salesman-to-be I did not yet realize that Bruce Benson was closing me, with the classic "feel-felt-found" that I would soon adopt to sell encyclopedias door-to-door.

"I have no interest in religion," I said emphatically. "I've seen the damage it's done in my family. I also really feel I'm agnostic.

There may or may not be a higher power. Truthfully, I don't know, and I really don't care."

"Do you know it is impossible for God to lie?" he said.

"What is that supposed to mean?"

"Just stating a fact that might be of comfort to you."

"How's that?"

"Well, you said you've seen the damage religion has done to your family, as the basis for not being interested."

"Correct."

"But those are all earthly constructs, and 'the truth' is about God, so if it's impossible for God to lie, how can that be anything but joyous? God will never betray you."

"Thank you, but I've heard it all before. I'm not interested. I need to go study."

"I'll come by again," Bruce said.

"That won't be necessary."

Bruce Benson just nodded and smiled, and I knew from watching my mom that he was coming back to see me inside of seven days, despite my objections.

AS I'd gotten older and neared the end of high school, I'd had less interaction with my father—other than what was required since I worked for him at his grocery store. The overt physical abuse had tailed off by then, but it was not entirely done; there were times that he would hit me and my brother Lee when we got into spats at the grocery store. One time Lee and I got into a knock-down, drag-out fight in the bakery while my younger brother, Dean, was waiting on a customer. Dean was scooping donuts into a bag for one of our regular customers, Mrs. Bayland, who was in her eighties, when the bakery pans started flying over the counter and making a tremendous racket, which caused our dad to run over from the other end of the store to break up our fight. He threw us into separate corners and proceeded to finish the beating. As usual, my beating was worse.

At 16, I worked at his store in Anchorage, on the other side of the tracks in a bad part of town. To further insulate myself from my family, I spent that summer living in the store. I had a mattress and stereo set up in the back near the stacked boxes of product inventory, where the smell of musty cardboard permeated my sleep. At the end of the summer I went back to Palmer to finish out high school.

I had loved living in the store on my own that summer so much that back in Palmer I rented a tiny studio apartment for $40 a month. After school, I worked from 3:30 to 8:30 p.m., then from 9 a.m. to 8:30 p.m. on Saturday and 8:30 a.m. to 6 p.m. on Sunday. I stocked shelves, swept floors, bagged groceries, and wheeled them out and loaded them into our customers' cars.

We had an alcoholic German baker named Ernie Geiger who created delectable pastries, cookies, and cakes that filled the store with wonderful smells. But the sweet aromas would mix together with that ubiquitous stench of cardboard boxes, a commingled odor I came to hate. To this day I don't like going into grocery stores, because it triggers that musty box smell in my mind.

One of the magazines we sold was called *Sexology*, which I would sneak into the front of my pants and read in the small bathroom with the door locked. Eventually my dad would be knocking on the door and yelling at me to get out there. *Go get your work done!* I had to sneak the magazine back onto the rack.

At some point my dad added a drive-through window where people could order burgers and drinks. We offered the mama burger, papa burger, and baby burger, or all three for $1.50. We called it the *Three Bears* drive-in. Dad would yell, "Someone at the drive-through!" and either Lee or I would have to drop what we were doing to man the window.

No question, my dad taught us how to work. When you got tired, he reminded you that your body wasn't as tired as you thought, that it was just your mind playing tricks. He may have been right, but I remember getting so tired—because I was either in school or working non-stop without breaks—that I would go into the bathroom and fall asleep on the grimy floor. I worked fifty hours a week, on top of my school and homework demands, and earned $86 every two weeks. It was that money that allowed me to get my little place in Palmer and live on my own until I graduated high school in 1966.

I was the valedictorian of my class and delivered the valedictorian address. I don't know if my father even came to the ceremony, because he never mentioned the accomplishment, let alone congratulated me. I had earned two college scholarships, one each from Sears Roebuck and Company and Montgomery Ward, which paid for my tuition and dorm for four years at University of Alaska in Fairbanks. My high school girlfriend, Colleen Patterson, headed to Methodist University in Anchorage. Off we went to two different campuses to expand our horizons.

AS predicted, within seven days Bruce Benson appeared again at my dorm room door with his pleasant smile and gentle demeanor. He was clutching more copies of *Watchtower* and *Awake*. I glanced up from the dull textbook I'd been staring at, took in the sight of him, and inexplicably said, "I have a lot of issues and anger."

"Let's talk about it," Bruce Benson said, moving across the door threshold and into my personal space for the first time. Then we sat on my bed and talked for the next four hours about life, my family upbringing, God, and religion.

Bruce had a way of getting me to keep opening up more and going deeper. He must have said his go-to phrase a hundred times that day: *I understand. I can see the pain.* The young man knew how to offer cool water to someone dying of thirst. He understands! *And* he can see the pain! My pain. A lot of pain I'd only ever carried by myself. What a relief. That felt really good, because no one else had ever understood. No one else had ever offered such comfort and empathy. It felt liberating to unload and share the burden I'd been carrying my entire life. But there was one secret I couldn't share with him, or anyone else. Not ever.

From that first long conversation, we began studying the Bible together. Bruce Benson would drop by with his JW magazines, and we'd plop on the bed and pick up where we'd left off. He explained that it wasn't the religion that was the problem. The issue was the way my father reacted to everything. That second part, at least, made a lot of sense. We studied from a book with a green cover titled *It is Impossible for God to Lie*. Clever guy, this Bruce Benson: He had told me that the first day we met.

Two things started to soften my opposition. First, Bruce told me JWs opposed any warfare, and that many were sitting in jail for refusing their draft call-ups to Vietnam. They were willing to stand up for their beliefs at any cost. The second thing was the promise of paradise on Earth.

After a few months of studying together, he took me with him to the congregation. Every person I met was kind and welcoming. Coming from a background of being emotionally and physically abused, when I was welcomed into a new, loving family I quickly bonded with them. For the first time in my life, it felt like I had a real family. This sense of belonging and a deep connection to a family were like oxygen I needed to survive. Part of that survival would be picking up the new rule book I would need to learn and follow to stay in this new family. It would take me decades to understand that having a sense of family, combined with my rigid adherence to rules, would also keep me anchored to a church community even as doing so started to conflict with who I really was.

I began to attend meetings, and soon they invited me to a JW convention. In my biology class, as we studied anatomy, the divine human design really got me wondering… maybe there was a God? How else to explain the intricacies of our human bodies and the magical way everything worked. I completed my first semester at University of Alaska with a 3.6 GPA and was looking forward to spring semester 1967.

As I continued attending services at the congregation, studying with Bruce, and exploring this path, a new delineation began to appear everywhere in the JW teachings: One was either of the world (ungodly) or of "the truth" (godly—obviously the preferred path). Being a college student put me in the former camp, as an ungodly miscreant. The first time I heard this I laughed aloud and immediately rejected it. What kind of crazy religion would dissuade earned knowledge and higher learning? In other words, what a ridiculous rule to expect people to follow. However, as I was surrounded more and more by true believers, what once sounded preposterous moved slowly toward plausible. And I had come to believe that my new JW family would know what was best, because they truly loved me.

My foundational epiphany arose because of the Vietnam War. I was number eighty-three in the draft lottery, which meant almost-certain jungle duty. While I had a student deferment, I also knew with the war escalating I would likely get called up regardless. If I had been tapped by the U.S. Selective Service I would have fled to Canada, because I simply would not go kill human beings for any geopolitical or other purpose whatsoever. And on that point I was in lockstep with the Jehovah's Witnesses, who vehemently but peacefully oppose all warfare as unjust. I remember the insanity of a Catholic priest blessing the weapons our soldiers would use to slaughter people in Vietnam. He told them to go fight and kill not with hate in their hearts, but rather with love. *Kill with love in your heart?* (The JWs weren't the only organization with some rules that made no sense). That sounded truly sick to me.

That's how my foundational anti-war beliefs steadily led me from the agnostic who had at first firmly rejected Bruce Benson to being a curious student of Bible prophecies—and, within months, believing in Jehovah and "the truth" without reservation. I was surrounded by loving JW brothers and sisters. I dedicated my life to this new path, which included accepting their organizational rule book that went beyond what the Bible teaches. This was not a hasty overnight switch, but a thoughtful evolution that happened in a relatively short period of time after a lot of deep reflection and many hours of study. It was also an interesting emotional transfer I did not understand at the time, which was trading my family of origin and their rules for a new family and their rules. I found comfort in that structure.

The unspoken pressure started to mount as Bruce and others quietly mentioned that it would be difficult to be in college—a clearly worldly pursuit—and devote oneself to Jehovah. In other words, if I stayed in college I would be a "worldly man" and not a "spiritual man," and I wouldn't be able to be a full-time pioneer, which meant dedicating at least one hundred hours each month to preaching and teaching in the door-to-door ministry (in recent years, the JW organization has relaxed its rules on getting a college degree, but when I was in college, the pursuit was considered too worldly, and therefore unacceptable).

Well, as a dedicated people-pleaser and rule-follower, my decision became surprisingly easy. I remember the lightning bolt hit me on a snowy February night in 1967 in Fairbanks, as I was praying about which path to take: college or religion. In the silence of watching the snowfall from my dorm room window, I knew without hesitation that I needed to give up my scholarships and follow Jehovah. And if I was quitting college, I would lose my student draft deferment. So I couldn't just dabble in this new orientation; I would need to become a full-time minister to get a religious deferment. And to do that, I would first need to get baptized. In what would have been my second semester, as the spring temperatures rose ever so slightly, I shocked the college counselor when I showed up to announce that, at 19, I was giving up my scholarships, quitting college, and entering full-time ministry. Just like that, with my worldly college education out of the way, I went to get baptized. I gave up college to gain a family who comforted me in ways my family of origin never had.

On March 5, 1967, I stood before the pool in the middle of the stage at Kingdom Hall in Anchorage. The officiant asked a bunch of questions I had studied for incessantly.

Who is the one true God?
Jehovah!
Have you dedicated your life to serving Jehovah?
Yes!

Full submersion. Without doubt, I felt renewed at that moment as I officially became part of a new loving family. I believed with all my heart that I was doing the right thing. In hindsight, however, following that first rule and quitting college was one of the biggest mistakes I made in this lifetime. No amount of income or financial wealth has ever replaced what I gave up: the inherent value of an education, and the pride and accomplishment of earning a college degree. Nonetheless, I was on a wholly new path and didn't have time to look back.

My girlfriend Colleen wasn't having any of it. There, too, my new JW friends said those of us in "the truth" could not date a worldly person. Colleen was not a Witness, and therefore she was ungodly. When I followed that rule and broke up with her, she was crushed. Did I mention she was a knockout? Well, as evidence beyond my own biased fancy, she went on to become Miss Alaska, appeared on *The Tonight Show Starring Johnny Carson* and was also in the Rose Bowl parade, among many appearances. And how's this for irony: She later became a JW, married another man named Dan, and went into full-time ministry herself.

Three months after I'd dropped out, my dad found out what I had done: dumped my scholarships, dumped Miss Alaska, and dumped college altogether to go into full-time ministry. He did not speak to me for three years. No great loss there! Indeed, I took a certain twisted pleasure in this turn, that I was doing the very thing that most enraged my father. *Gotcha!* Concurrently, I had earned my mother's full approval. She could not have been more pleased that I had dropped the worldly pursuit of ivory-tower academia to join her among the JW faithful.

Freshly baptized and out of college, I stayed in Fairbanks, where the congregation built out a two-bedroom basement apartment Bruce and I could stay in as long as we continued pioneering. I worked part-time at a grocery store (no connection to my dad) and spent the rest of my time pioneering with Bruce. I wasn't allowed to pioneer full-time for one year, but in the meantime I could be a vacation pioneer, at seventy-five hours the first month, and one hundred hours every month thereafter. With Fairbanks as our base, Bruce and I would leave early Friday morning and drive several hundred miles north, crossing the Arctic Circle into rugged territory on rough dirt and gravel roads. We ventured to remote Inuit villages that were only accessible during the summer when the snow melted enough to allow passage. We'd stop at every random clapboard shack along the way, too, to spread "the truth." During the summer, our work was never limited by daylight, because even at midnight it was still light out.

At "night," which was just a few hours of purplish twilight, Bruce and I pitched a tent and camped on the banks of beautiful rivers in northern Alaska. I've since traveled the world, and the Alaskan wilderness is still the most gorgeous natural scenery I have ever witnessed (although the swarms of giant mosquitoes often made Bruce and me question our sanity). With the river waters gurgling nearby, we'd grill hamburgers or hot dogs over our campfire. For breakfast, we'd rebuild the fire to make scrambled eggs, ham, and a hot pot of hobo coffee, which was a steel pot stirred with water, grounds, and no filter.

During the day we visited the Inuits who lived in wooden huts in numerous different villages. We also encountered "homesteaders," who had lived on their property long enough to legally claim it from the state of Alaska as their own. Many of them were also called "sourdoughs," the local term for people who were sour on Alaska, but didn't have the dough to leave. The rustic location made for a rough life, but the people were always welcoming. I had a new religion and a new family, including Bruce, so I was as happy as a tick.

The Inuit were hunters and salmon fishermen who lived in modest huts. They didn't know anything of our white man's God Jehovah, or of Jesus Christ. They followed traditional Inuit religious practices, including animism and shamanism, with healers mediating with spirits. We met one elderly grandmother who was basically toothless; she had been deemed no longer useful and put outside where she could pass away peacefully. When a new baby came along, the family put the toothless infant outside with the grandmother too. The grandmother told them babies were born like that, without teeth. She assured them teeth would come in eventually, and the baby would be fine. They were surprised by this news and took the baby back in, along with the grandmother because of her great wisdom. Many of these people had never been more than walking distance from their birthplace. Whenever an airplane flew overhead, we had to explain that those machines were carrying people and goods around the state of Alaska. I'm not sure which explanation engineered more confused looks: Jehovah, or modern aviation. Mostly we left behind literature, including *Watchtower* and *Awake* magazines as well as a series of books and brochures. The idea was to leave enough reading material to keep them occupied until someone returned the next summer. Over a few days we'd place about 150 pieces of literature, all of which we recorded on our field service report.

After pioneering with Bruce for about a year, I moved back to Anchorage, where I lived with a married JW couple who took me in. I would spend the next five years working full-time in ministry, as a JW pioneer. Since I was an ordained minister, I tried to equate that status, and rationalize my new standing, as equivalent to earning my college degree.

Of course, I had no idea that finding religion was simply a

way for me to further bury the secret I still carried. At that point, about two years before I would show up unannounced at Snelling and Snelling to take ownership of "my job," I believed that as I became more and more successful at being a Jehovah's Witness, I would fix everything. In other words, I was finally on a track to rectify, and eventually erase, that dark part of me that was so abhorrent, the secret I would have to guard until my death.

And at the time I was fully onboard with my mom's thinking, because Bruce Benson had led me to this wonderful new family I'd never had. In the congregation, everyone was kind, accepting (at least of the version of me I let them see), and loving (as long as you were abiding by all their rules).

Finally, I thought, I had found my true family and a real home.

Part 2

Success

Eight

I Locked It All Down

WHEN I WAS 7 YEARS OLD, I KNEW I LIKED BOYS. I first acted on it when I was 13. I didn't act on it again until I was 70. In between I lived a lifetime of fear, shame, and hiding.

The shame was because I believed I was flawed. I was no good. My inner construct was damaged, and when something was broken beyond repair you just threw it away. Suicide was one way to throw away a life. Another way was work. My dad taught me two things: judgment and anger. And, by default, he gave me the work ethic that would make me a millionaire. If I wasn't a normal man, at least it was normal for a man to work all the time.

When I was born in 1947, homosexuality was categorized as a mental health issue; it was officially deemed deviant. I never chose to like boys. I actually tried to convince myself I was bisexual, because even that was easier than being gay. Some attraction to women meant I had some strands of normalcy inside me; to be gay was to be one hundred percent abnormal and deviant.

Especially in the Eisenhower years in America, in the fifties, and then into the simultaneously button-down and turbulent sixties. And I still believe my father would have killed me if he had ever found out I was gay.

When I first suspected I liked boys, at age 7, I would wrestle with the neighborhood boys my age. I didn't know what "gay" meant. I would have dreams as a young boy where the Lone Ranger would chase me, both of us racing along on horses, and then he'd tackle me off my horse. My dad never talked to me about the facts of life. My mom told the three of us boys in one sentence, without any follow-up questions allowed: *A man takes his penis and sticks it in a woman, and that's how babies are made.* While scientifically accurate, the dissertation left out all the important steps between insertion and birth. In the coming years I started puberty, a confusing time when my nipples got hard. I did not know what was happening, and thought I was getting some strange illness or disease. I also had nocturnal emissions, and didn't know what the hell was happening except that those felt good. Still, I had guilt, because somehow it seemed like I was doing something wrong and nobody told me otherwise. If the duty for any discussion with the sons fell to my dad, he never said a word.

When I went to middle school I wanted to be a cheerleader, which was also unusual for a male in the fifties. I tried out, made the squad, and was a cheerleader in seventh grade. I never told my dad or mom, because I was embarrassed. Going to the locker room, looking at my classmates in various states of undress, was exciting and unnerving. What if someone caught my secret glances? And, yet, I was attracted to them and could not stop myself from looking, especially the ninth-graders who were further into puberty and even more attractive. When I wasn't in the locker room, I spent a lot of seventh grade fantasizing about seeing those ninth-graders.

Of course, extreme feelings clouded these longings: I was

guilty because it was all wrong. I was ashamed. I remember when I was cheerleading, a group of boys a little older than I was confronted me and were about to beat me up when I somehow talked them out of it. The reason for the threat of physical violence? Because it was just wrong for a boy to be a cheerleader. My talent did count for something: As the first cheerleader to do a flip, I was always popular with the girls, which helped nudge me back toward normalcy.

The first time I acted on my innate impulses was in 1960, when I was 13. We had moved to Soldotna, Alaska, on the Kenai Peninsula, after I finished seventh grade. By then Dad was still in the grocery business and running his own stores; he dubbed them B & B Super, which had nothing to do with the family surname: it stood for Better Buys. Dad bought a Piggly Wiggly in Palmer and renamed it B & B Super. I would hone my work ethic in the aisles, bakeries, and stockrooms of Dad's grocery stores all through high school. It was the start of my love for work, as an escape, even as my hatred of my father hardened. By then he was unredeemable, a thought that gives me great sadness. He was, after all, my one and only father.

That first sexual experience was with my best friend, who was a year older. We went bowling and then to his house for a planned sleepover—except we ended up in the same bed. I initiated the physical contact, which he totally enjoyed. I was so ashamed, though, about what I'd done that I pulled back completely and pretended to be asleep. Immediately the shame overwhelmed me. This was a transgression from which I would never recover. I was evil. I'd never do that again—which was not entirely true, but was a promise that held for fifty-seven years.

My best friend and I never acknowledged, let alone talked about, what had happened. The guilt was horrifying. I dealt with severe depression afterward, and Mom's heavy religious underpinning left me feeling perverted. I was the damaged goods I heard other people mocking. A queer. Fairy. Homo.

So I locked it all down. Of course I always noticed men, but I self-corrected by reprimanding myself with shame. I'd worked harder and continually prayed to God to dismiss it. I kept my mind so busy I squeezed out any possibility of a spare moment to face myself. My addictions kept me distracted: work, religion, and exercise.

I gritted my teeth from 1960 until 2017, through two marriages to women and a career on the telephone, without being physical with a man again until I was 70 years old.

Nine

A Sobering Reality

WHEN I WAS 6 YEARS OLD I SAW MY MOTHER CRYING after a nasty fight she'd had with my dad. I could hear them yelling. I felt compelled, somehow, to comfort her. I told her I would go out, get a job, and support her financially. Obviously, at age 6 this was a promise I could not fulfill.

I was a boy who got his start in life with a father who was at best indifferent, and who I believe truly didn't like me. I absorbed that same energy and struggled for years with not liking myself. From an early age, carrying the toxic shame of knowing I was gay in an unaccepting time—in the late fifties and sixties—only solidified my self-loathing. I'd never be normal, which meant I'd never be good enough. Not for myself, and not for anyone else. I would never measure up to whatever standard I was supposed to achieve, and so I was inherently "less than."

Looking back, by the day I promised my mother I would support her, my template was already set in reinforced concrete:

I would spend the rest of my life taking care of everyone else, *anyone* else but myself—so I didn't have to deal with the shame of being gay. Dan the People-Pleaser was officially born. And when combined with the legendary persistence and work ethic I was destined to unleash on an unsuspecting June Wells at Snelling and Snelling, I would turn my people-pleasing into a high art form. In other words, I would overachieve at people-pleasing just as I would overachieve at work and religion, all to mask the pain of not being able to accept myself.

I unconsciously developed a strategy: When I gave people something—a compliment, advice, money, gifts, answers to problems, loans… it didn't matter what—I was able to direct the focus away from me. So Dan the People-Pleaser led the way, to keep the Real Dan squarely in the murky shadows of his dark closet. Except that, like an addict chasing the dragon, pleasing and overachieving never led me to accept myself. The only answer was to redouble my efforts and go harder, faster, and longer than anyone else around me. Because if I paused, even for a second, someone might glimpse the real me. And that someone might be me.

As a kid who came of age in the fifties and sixties, my somewhat twisted emotional construct had an enormous upside: The combination of wanting to do well for others and my iron-will work ethic made me a born salesman in the golden age of door-to-door selling. In a time before online shopping delivered everything straight to one's front door, people had to trudge to local department stores. Door-to-door salesmen were the prehistoric version of Amazon, the early analog version of delivering wares directly to people's houses. The demographics of the sixties meant most men were at work while the women stayed home to wrangle the children and run the household. Enter a whole host of products targeted directly at homemakers and sold by men (yes, almost exclusively men, in crisp suits and ties), such as the Fuller Brush Man who lugged around cleaning supplies and hairbrushes, solvents, silver polish, and personal care products.

How much easier to buy direct from the well-dressed salesman (who made sure to let you know during his pitch that he, too, had hungry mouths to feed) than piling in the land barge and heading to Montgomery Ward. By my time as a teenager in the sixties, the Fuller Brush Company had become an American institution. And my family of origin had already imprinted in me the very skills to succeed on the front lines of selling.

Following behind the Fuller Brush Man, knocking doors a day or two later, might be a vacuum cleaner salesman selling the finest machines available, including Kirby, Electrolux, Hoover, and Eureka. These salesmen were all skilled pitch artists who dragged the heavy machines right into living rooms and brought their own bags of dirt to wow their prospects. Sure, they sold vacuum cleaners that weighed as much as a Volkswagen, but they would last forever.

And of course, every kid who grew up in the fifties, sixties, and even seventies needed a good set of encyclopedias at home — the precursor to today's online search engines. Without a good set of encyclopedias, you either needed to have a friend whose parents had sprung for a set, or be ready to go to the library to complete that school writing assignment on the big cats of Africa. The first edition of the Encyclopedia Britannica was published and printed in Edinburgh, Scotland, in 1768. The first edition of the World Book Encyclopedia came along in 1917 (as simply World Book), with a clear advantage over Britannica: World Book was more user-friendly by design, less formal, and less technical. And it would be salesmen in suits selling encyclopedias to women in their living rooms while their husbands were at work. It was the perfect product for me: one I believed in, sold in perhaps the most challenging way as a door-to-door salesman and on a one-hundred commission basis. A better scenario could not have existed for an overachieving people-pleaser to begin a career in sales.

My illustrious career as a door-to-door salesman along the icy streets of Boise, Idaho, began after my new wife and I moved from

Alaska. After Eileen Keaton became Eileen Bolen on February 24, 1968, we spent our honeymoon in Soldotna, Alaska, where I hunched over a stack of musty boxes (ugh, the smell!) at the back of my dad's grocery store, writing letters as part of my one hundred hours per month of pioneer time for the JW church. Yes, I really knew how to woo my new bride: ministry in the back of a grocery store. Eileen was bored by the exercise, so she walked across the street under the falling snow to see what was playing at the movie theater, which was in a Quonset hut. When she slipped and ended up on her butt in the middle of the street, I started laughing hysterically!

The biggest honeymoon highlight, beyond the fully authorized and approved sex I was thoroughly enjoying, was going out to dinner one night with one of Dad's employees, Doyle Jowers, who ran that store in Soldotna. All I remember from that dinner is asking Doyle: how in the world did he get his teeth so brilliantly white?

"I brush with Bon Ami," he replied between bites, as though the revelation was the most normal thing in the world.

In Anchorage, we lived in a dank basement apartment, a one-bedroom that was as cheap as it was small. There was one permanently smudged window where we could see people's legs and feet as they walked by. There was a long set of slick cement stairs, too, that Eileen fell all the way down, from top to bottom. Thankfully she was all right, but I burst out laughing again — I can't control myself when people fall, which I find endlessly hilarious.

As I began my pioneering on behalf of Jehovah, James Milton was the branch overseer for Jehovah's Witnesses for the entire state of Alaska. His wife, Donna Milton, whose maiden name was Slob, also worked at the branch office. We affectionately called Donna and her sister the Slob Sisters.

Eileen had a job at Safeway, as a waitress, while I did my full-time ministry work. I had gone from being a college student who lived above ground and dated Miss Alaska, a young man finally free from the dogma and dysfunction of my youth, to being a college dropout and full-time minister who lived underground and had voluntarily given himself over to the same dogma he once abhorred. But I was truly happy, and on the path I believed to be my destiny—dedicating my life to Jehovah. Pioneering just seemed like what I should be doing. To get hours, I'd go by myself and knock on doors. On one of those calls a dog attacked me. The owner came out, retrieved her dog, and left me bleeding in her driveway without so much as a "hello." I still have scars on my right arm from that day, and I still fear unknown dogs.

This is when the earliest fissures started to appear in my marriage, the first faint lines of addictive tendencies in my new bride. When we got married, Eileen had a small debt on a credit card from Lerner's, a women's clothing store. We had very little money, and I certainly didn't have any credit cards, but the small debt seemed innocuous and was one we would be able to pay off without too much strain. Also, when we first met, when Eileen paraded around in her white go-go boots, neither of us ever drank alcohol. After we married, Eileen began drinking wine—but, again, what harm was there in a glass or two of wine?

Meanwhile, the harsh weather of the great frontier of Alaska was wearing us down. And just to back up a bit: Why in the world had my father ever moved us there in the first place? He had heard the 1960 hit song recorded by Johnny Horton, *North to Alaska*, which was featured in the movie of the same name. When that song got stuck in Dad's head, there was no turning back. The Albertsons where he worked in Twin Falls burned to the ground, and after they'd rebuilt the store, Dad managed it for several months. Then he decided he wanted to strike out on his own after hearing the Johnny Horton song. Shortly after, he piled his wife and us six kids into a camper and we took off for Alaska. We drove the Alcan Highway from Dawson Creek, British Columbia, to Delta Junction, Alaska, which at the time was 595 miles of dirt, gravel, and grime.

Along the way, we'd squat on a portable toilet in the camper that had plastic bags to catch our waste. When one of us used it the first time and asked Dad what to do with the full bag, he nonchalantly said without hesitation, "Just toss it out back." For six children, this became the highlight of the trip, tossing our bags of urine and feces out the back of the camper as Dad soldiered on North to Alaska. On one unfortunate occasion, when we went to throw one of the bags, it slipped open and came blowing back into the camper. The bag hit the camper floor and splattered us three Bolen boys.

Dad set up his first grocery store in Soldotna, and also bought a crab boat he worked for a few years during the summers. Crabbing was similar to the grocery business: hard work and no money. He'd take us fishing to Moose Creek, where we could (legally) snag silver salmon about as fast as we could reset our hooks. Although we enjoyed the outdoor pursuits, the weather was brutal.

AS a newlywed couple, Eileen and I decided to move to Idaho, where our daughter Tiffany was born. After she came along, we moved to our house on Victory Road in the Boise suburb of Meridian, which was plopped in the middle of a cow pasture. Each morning we got up to see the cows staring at us, but for eighty dollars a month we didn't care. Soon came my job at Sears Roebuck and Company, and the ambush interview I deployed at Snelling and Snelling.

But my first job in Idaho was in the selling trenches as a door-to-door salesman of World Book encyclopedias and the companion Cyclo-Teacher, which World Book produced as a teaching aid to stimulate learning. The Cyclo-Teacher came in a large box with an elaborate system of two-sided, color-coded wheels in six subjects: study skills, mathematics, language arts, social studies, vocabulary, and activities. This job was a straight commission gig: I got a percentage of each $300 set of encyclopedias I sold, and also a part of each Cyclo-Teacher. Most weeks I could sell two sets of encyclopedias. Since my aged Oldsmobile was still stuck in Alaska because I didn't have the money to have it shipped, I spent the mornings trudging through the snow on foot with my World Book wares, and the afternoons selling my religion to earn my pioneer hours. I didn't enjoy selling encyclopedias, but almost immediately I was good at it. I'd already picked up what would become a classic selling model: feel-felt-found.

"Thank you, but I'm not interested," a smiling housewife would say as a child peered out from behind her.

"You must have a good reason for that," I'd say.

"They have a set at his school," she'd answer.

Bingo: feel-felt-found. "I understand why you feel that way. Many of the people I talk to each day have felt the same way. If I may, let me tell you what I've found: I think you're going to see this makes a big difference in your children's grades at school, and in their lives."

I was selling knowledge in the morning and religion in the afternoon. I always dressed in a suit or a sports jacket and tie (same as when I did my ministry). Of course, six months of the year, I would also be bundled in a puffy down jacket and earmuffs.

Whatever I was selling, I knew I had to knock on doors. Lugging a few sample volumes of World Book encyclopedias and a Cyclo-Teacher was rough, especially in the bad weather. But my wife was pregnant at the time, had already had two miscarriages and couldn't work. I had to provide for my family. Just like my dad taught me: whatever needed to be done. Just like the 6-year-old had promised his mom. I had a tremendous drive from day one, because I liked people and I liked selling. When I made a sale the customer paid a deposit, and then weeks later the set of encyclopedias would arrive at their house. I don't know how many of us there were in the sixties, but by 1978 World Book had a sales force of 60,000 people. Even in the late eighties, the World

Book sales force still had 45,000 door-to-door representatives. I'm proud that for almost a year I was part of that shining era of the American door-to-door salesman, and was providing a unique and legendary product.

As I said earlier, we didn't even have a car. We barely had enough money to buy food. When Tiffany came along on June 22, 1969, it was life-changing. *Oh my God!* I was a full-time (unpaid) minister without a stable job. *Am I going to be able to take care of this child?* I was 22 years old. These were the supposed "Last Days," because the world was coming to an end. This JW tenet came from the combined forces of Bible prophecies and the widespread unrest of the late sixties. Officially I believed it, because the world condition did seem precarious. However, unofficially I also wondered whether all the nations were actually going to rise against other nations, followed by Armageddon. I mostly focused on what I could control: my own ministry and connecting with the people, my new family, I met through those activities. Without my new family, I would be alone. For example, I became a spiritual leader for Chris Watson, who was fifteen years younger than I was and had had a rough upbringing. He was just one of the many JWs I developed a strong connection with. Those deep bonds of love were something I'd never experienced in my own family of origin. The JWs were indeed my new family.

Economic necessity led me to Sears—a small step up in terms of stability over selling encyclopedias door to door—and then to Snelling and Snelling. Even once onboard there, I was still pioneering for one hundred hours every month, which was knocking on doors, preaching, and teaching. Some of the precepts of my work life and spiritual life did not align. The church admonished us to simplify and not reach out for the goods of the world. Instead we were to do more for Jehovah, because, again, it was two minutes to midnight, or the end of times. But at work, I quickly rose to the top of the Snelling and Snelling roster. The reality was that I had a wife and child to support. I loved my daughter, but from the time she was born, I sacrificed time with her during those early years. Eileen took physical care of Tiffany, and they became emotionally bonded in a way I missed because I was always working and pioneering. I regret that I missed that time in my daughter's life. Later, at Management Recruiters, I would take Tiffany with me to the office on Saturday afternoons after my preaching and teaching in the morning. She would sit in the chairs, spin, and clank away on the typewriter keys, but that was more so I could work rather than spending meaningful time as father and daughter.

By age 24, I was an elder in the congregation. Elder status came after serving as a ministerial servant, one of the worker bees of the congregation, and after meeting various requirements including regular meeting attendance and field service activity. Again, I was an overachiever, but also a good speaker who drew people in and developed strong rapport. As an elder, one of my responsibilities was to serve on three-person judicial committees whenever a serious sin had been committed: adultery, immorality, drug use, major theft, alcoholism, and others transgressions. Ironic that I would sit in self-righteous judgment of my fellow congregation members, even as I buried my own fatal secret that would have had me immediately disfellowshipped by our standards if I ever acted on it.

Looking back, I believe I buried my truth so deep within that I was homophobic, espousing the thinking of the day that gay people were abnormal, and I was never to associate with them. Meanwhile, I still noticed men and found them attractive. Talk about deep denial. But as a church elder in the sixties and seventies, it was a matter of self-preservation, because being a male homosexual was about the worst thing you could be, spiritually, morally, and even legally. So what better way to avoid ever thinking about that than by staying busy 24/7?

In addition to long hours at Snelling and Snelling, I dedicated four other days each week to my religious activities. On Tuesday evenings I led a study group at the Kingdom Hall, which required hours of advance preparation and study on my own. Thursday evenings were reserved for theocratic ministry school, where again I was the ministry school overseer leading a small group of students. The JW organization would develop themes and organize the material we would study, such as "What is Babylon the Great?" or "Why is God called the Ancient of Days?" We followed the discussions those evenings with another meeting, called a service meeting, that dealt with topics provided by the JW organization on how to be more effective in the ministry.

On Saturday mornings I hit the streets to knock on doors (ministry work) and then usually went to the office Saturday afternoons to catch up on paperwork and plan the next week. Sunday mornings, of course, included the 10 a.m. public talk at the congregation, given by one of us elders on a rotating basis. Then at 11 a.m. we had a one-hour *Watchtower* study, which I would sometimes conduct. In total, on top of my work hours I was spending at least twenty hours a week on ministry work and preparing for my various talks and study groups. My life was the church and work, without a spare moment for anything else. Clearly I was addicted to both my religion and my work. It was easy to get lost in both, because these were my genuine passions: I loved people, and everything I did in my ministry and my job revolved around people. Meeting people. Conversing with people. Teaching people, and learning from people. Convincing people to buy what I was selling. Watching people react well to whatever they'd just purchased, whether it was God or a new job opportunity. At that time I believed I'd found the truth in what religion was teaching, but concurrently ignored some deep concerns I had with the JW organization. Why? Because I felt I had also found the so-called perfect family and the so-called perfect religion. If I ever did raise a concern or question about the official dogma, the JWs always had an answer: "Everyone questions it at first; just pray for more understanding." Or, "You can question it, but over time you'll come to accept it."

Drip, drip, drip. The messaging was always steady, consistent, and constantly reinforced.

What I didn't fully understand or acknowledge was that my passions became more important than my family, because just being good wasn't good enough: I had to be number one at the church. I had to be number one at work. I had to be the best at whatever I did. My overachieving brought results—and, most importantly, the recognition I craved.

That Dan Bolen is really great!

It's easy to see, then, why I missed what had started to happen at home with Eileen while I was gone all the time. Eileen was very outgoing and flamboyant. She dressed with sparkles and was the life of any party. She was very complimentary of others. She had an undeniable appeal, which is what drew me in that day I saw her at the grocery store in the white go-go boots. But now, while I was at work or with the congregation, Eileen was at home enjoying her wine. What started as a glass or two steadily increased. She drank Gallo wine we purchased in gallon jugs. I would join her on the weekends for a glass or two, but I had no idea she was hiding the amount she was drinking during the week. I was so consumed with my religion and work that it was easy for me to miss what might have been warning signs.

Exactly how many gallon jugs of wine were we buying each week?

After I'd moved on from Snelling and Snelling to take the job at Dunhill, things came to a head on a trip we took with my parents. My dad had invited Eileen, Tiffany, and me to go to Canada with him and my mom in their motorhome. It had all the markers of a bad *North to Alaska!* redux. My first thought was that a motorhome vacation with my father was way too close for comfort—to be stuck with my dad in a confined space. My second thought made me giggle: I wondered if we'd be tossing our bags of waste out the back while he drove. In the end, I went along with the trip idea. The main reason I agreed to go was for my daughter: I didn't want to deny her the chance to at least know her grandparents. So off we went, once again, North to Alaska!, which this time was really Canada.

One night on the trip we stopped to camp, Dad started drinking, and things quickly unraveled when he mumbled, "You quit college…" and then went on to be vindictive, belittling, and insulting.

"Let it go," Eileen whispered.

"I'm OK," I said, taking deep breaths and using all my energy to not react. However, he was unrelenting—just as he had been when I was a child. I was conditioned to accept abuse by my dad. When I was with him as a child, I did not have a voice; I was not allowed. And when I did assert myself by standing up to him, I just got more abuse. Even though I hated him, I knew I had to play by the rules. Otherwise, I knew there would be more pain.

On this trip, on top of his needling was all the pressure that had been building in me from over-working, over-preaching, and over-stuffing my hidden shame I had not yet shared with anyone. I exploded in a rage that shocked me as I screamed at him. It began with, "You son of a bitch…" and went on and on, including all the labels I thought he needed to hear: narcissist, alcoholic, bad father, bad husband, etc. My mom was horrified. My wife was horrified. Tiffany was only 5, so she didn't fully understand what was happening. I'm not sure what I was feeling, but my rage ended with, "I'm not putting up with this shit anymore from you. We're done with this trip, and I'm done with you!"

I wanted to destroy my dad, and I felt like I had. We grabbed our bags and walked out of the motorhome. Then I started sobbing. All the anger I'd been holding back for a lifetime had just been unleashed on my father, who probably deserved a lot of it but certainly not all. Some good chunk of what I'd just dumped on him was mine to own. Soon my parents were slow-rolling behind us in the motorhome, my mom begging us to get back in and come back to the campsite.

"No," I said. "Not with him. I'm done."

We found a roadside motel, checked in and booked flights back to Boise. Then I started crying again. After we got back home and my parents were back in their home in Mississippi, my initial relief of unloading all my toxic rage was replaced with a deep guilt. He was still my dad, after all. And I prided myself on being the bigger man despite his shortcomings. I was an elder in my congregation: I felt compelled to offer some grace. I waited about a month before calling home.

"He doesn't want to talk to you," my mom said. So I got a flight to Mississippi, went to their house and sat down with him.

"I said horrible things to you. I hope you'll forgive me."

He said nothing. I wasn't sure what to feel. I was glad I had apologized, for myself, so whether he accepted my gesture or not was less important. Then I just felt sad again, that this was the only father I would ever get, and we were back to where we always went: him silent and ignoring me, and me just wanting some small gesture of acknowledgment that I existed at all, that I was worthy to be in his space.

At that moment a cloying heat flashed through my body, and I just wanted to get out of there as fast as possible. I could not even acknowledge to myself what was happening inside: that I had just realized that somehow I had become my father, the man I despised. This was a tough pill to swallow, that I was just like my old man: not a good father to my own daughter. I certainly didn't abuse her, but I neglected her because I was always either working as a recruiter or serving Jehovah. And that was the truth, and it was heartbreaking.

My own family, Eileen and Tiffany, had become secondary to me.

Ten

A Sobering Reality

THE LAST TIME I SAW MY YOUNGER BROTHER, Dean, he was choking me at his daughter's wedding. It was 1993, in metropolitan Phoenix, during the final downward spiral of my own marriage to Eileen. I had been talking to Dean's ex-wife, which was apparently what triggered his rage. He had been drinking, of course, which fanned the flames of his generalized anger. Sadly, none of us three Bolen boys had yet learned to step outside the footprint of our father and his base orientation to rage. Confronting my own anger would be one of my greatest challenges.

For me, there was a clear line back to our father, who both overtly and subconsciously taught us to be angry. I'm not blaming him, but I carry his DNA. I could get angry quite quickly. Unlike my father, my anger never escalated to any physical abuse of anyone, and for that I was always grateful. But anger was still a problem I had to monitor and control. When I did overreact to someone with anger I usually caught myself, apologized, and admitted to them that my behavior had been wrong. Whenever I slipped into those angry expressions, I was left with the lingering shame of the knee-jerk outburst—behaving just like my dad.

It was a sobering reality to piece together over the years: that as I simultaneously harbored deep hatred toward my father, I also had to admit I often operated just like him in this one realm. That epiphany made me feel like a piece of garbage. It would be decades before I would start to figure out this puzzle and make progress at doing better. Then, as I reconfigured my own inner reality, I would eventually be drawn to people who were gentle souls. But long before that progress, back when Bill Clinton was just starting his first term as U.S. president and gasoline was just a little over a buck a gallon, I was painfully reminded how it felt to be on the receiving end of the dark Bolen rage—at the hands of my own brother.

I was able to separate myself from Dean and breathe again, thanks to Chris Watson, the friend I'd met in Meridian, Idaho, who was like a son to me. He helped pull Dean off me.

"Anyone who comes after you, Danny, will have to go through me first," Chris told me. I was in shock, and retreated to our hotel room.

Coincidentally, the very next weekend was Tiffany's wedding in a Kingdom Hall in La Quinta, California. I called Dean and told him not to come. If he did show up I promised to call the police, report the choking incident, and press charges. He was defiant, but also knew I was serious; as I suspected he would, he heeded my warning and stayed away. The night at Dean's daughter's wedding was the last time I saw my younger brother. He and I did not speak to each other again for eighteen years, until he called me from Mexico in 2011. He had gone to live there in a final desperate attempt to outrun his demons: alcoholism, rage, deceit, and the abuse of others.

"I was successful at your company, Danny," he said. He wasn't wrong; he had been my top producer (just behind me) and one of the best Management Recruiters account executives in the entire nation. On that phone call, however, I could tell immediately that the drugs and alcohol had addled Dean's brain to the point that he believed his glory days had been just a few years prior, and he'd easily be able to knock off the rust and get right back at it. In truth, the time he was talking about had been more than three decades earlier, when he was a completely different person. By 2011, in mind, body, and spirit Dean was never going to be that same successful man again.

"And so," he said, "I'm ready to go back to work for you. I just wanted to ask if you would consider hiring me back?"

I was shocked, then shocked a little more, and then beyond shocked. The last time I'd seen him, eighteen years prior, he'd choked me, a crime in all fifty states. He never apologized or did anything to make amends for that incident. Even worse—way worse—I'd since discovered he'd unleashed the darkest of his impulses, at various times, on one of our family members and my then pre-teenage daughter Tiffany. And now, after all that, including the worst betrayal a man could visit on his brother's child, he was calling to ask me for a job? When I found out what he had done to my family member and my daughter several years earlier, I wanted to kill him with a baseball bat, tapping into the exploding rage I had learned so well. But by then, in 2011, I had progressed—so what came out was civil, firm, and direct: "Absolutely not, Dean. You and I both know our relationship is over."

That was the last time I spoke to Dean, who had been one of my closest friends when we were kids. Within a week of that phone call he suffered a heart attack and died in Mexico. His Mexican girlfriend had taken him to the hospital, dropped him off, and taken off in his car, leaving him there to die. We were told we had forty-eight hours to get his body out of Mexico, or he would be buried there. His death left me reeling, and wondering how someone with so much promise had fallen so far.

Dean had a head start in life as the good-looking star athlete, with his basketball skills vaulting him into the good graces of our father. Dean also enjoyed a certain innate charisma that undeniably paved the way for him to ascend to the heights as my best producer at Management Recruiters. That was a different era, back when the Village People and Donna Summer ruled the charts, Jimmy Carter was in the White House, and Dean and I were grabbing the American dream.

Eleven

The FAB Sheet

ALMOST IMMEDIATELY AFTER LAUNCHING MY Management Recruiters franchise on Shoreline Drive, on November 8, 1976, I soared to the top of the national organization. In my first year I received accolades as an accredited, master, and professional account executive. But those markers were just a warm-up lap for what was to come. From 1977 until 1985 when I sold the business, I earned all the top distinctions *each* year (every designation was based on financial production) as part of the manager's club, VIP club, superstar club, and executive club. Word spread quickly throughout the company leadership ranks: *This new guy in Boise is making some noise, and hitting some production numbers that have never been hit before!* That was the key—the numbers—because the numbers didn't lie. I didn't go to Management Recruiters to be number one and win awards. Those wins happened because I loved the business, I loved people, and I had a knack for helping them solve their dilemmas, whether it was an employer seeking an employee or a candidate seeking an employer. Everyone won, including me.

In February 1979 I landed in the director's club with $250,000 in cumulative placements. From there my production only grew; I hit $500,000 in 1980 (president's club), $750,000 in 1981 (chairman's club), and then the $1 million hall of fame in 1982. I was the national producing manager of the year twice, and national manager of the year while competing among 600 Management Recruiters offices. All this success came out of our humble operation in Boise, Idaho, a market so small and uninteresting to Bob Anderson that he initially mistook the place for a one-gas-station town in Iowa. Riding shotgun with me through all that high-flying success, from 1977 to 1983, was my younger brother, Dean.

Without question, both brothers, Lee and Dean, had the legendary Bolen work ethic, maybe the only benevolent gift given by our father. Lee came to work for me for a short time. By the mid-seventies he was out of the U.S. Army after four years, and was eager to enjoy the same level of financial success he saw me achieving. I hired Lee in the early eighties and put him on a desk. He was determined and stubborn, like all of us Bolen boys, and he put in long hours as we all did. He followed every admonishment I hurled at him: *Overcome the objection! Respond to their question! Say something... anything! Ask for more data from the client. The only wrong question is the one you never ask.*

After his calls we would do a quick post-mortem. "He didn't tell me the target date," Lee would say.

"No," I said. "You didn't ask about their target date. It's not their job to tell you; it's your job to ask."

In the recruiting business, everything had to be sold twice: the employer on the candidate, and the candidate on the employer, which was no easy task. Lee did everything I asked, and carefully followed the blueprint I laid out. However, after a few months it became clear to us both that Lee just didn't have the right personality and skill set to shine. His work ethic was not the issue; but no matter how hard Lee worked, he just couldn't carry conversations on the phone. He was more the silent type, and still is to this day. Selling anything, whether encyclopedias, used cars, or recruitment services, requires a certain personality that Lee just doesn't have. I had to have a tough conversation and tell my older brother that professional recruiting just wasn't for him. He recommitted to the janitorial business he'd already started, and successfully ran that operation for decades. To this day, Lee and his wife (his high school sweetheart) still live in Boise where we worked together all those years ago.

Dean, on the other hand, was a natural right out of the gate, a born salesman who could talk to anyone with a smooth patter he didn't have to work to find. Dean could have worked the other side of the street during my door-to-door World Book selling days and come close to my sales totals. He had innate charisma and personality you can't teach. Dean's natural gifts worked within the Jehovah's Witnesses congregation, too, where he could break the rules without much punishment. Dean liked to smoke while playing golf, a no-no that could get one disfellowshipped. He hid his issues from the elders and stayed in their good graces because, after all, he was Dean Bolen. He and I lived fifteen minutes away from each other. Dean and his family had a house on a golf course, and by 1980 Eileen and I had upgraded and bought our first house, a brand-new home in Eagle Hills, which was also on a golf course.

To go along with the new house, I bought my first Mercedes-Benz sedan at Lyle Pearson Auto Group, which is still in operation to this day. My new car was white with a gray interior, and it created whispers within the JW congregation.

"You just don't see JWs driving a white Mercedes," a fellow parishioner said to me one Sunday morning as we walked toward the Kingdom Hall. Indeed, in the JW dogma anyone who pursued money was materialistic, and any good Jehovah's Witness was supposed to be above such petty worldly pursuits. Despite the ongoing whispers, I didn't let anyone dissuade me because I truly loved what I did. This was a delicate balance because the avowed rule follower was ignoring a JW rule.

I justified my worldly path because I wasn't motivated to pursue money; I pursued my career because I loved talking to people and solving their problems. In return, I was well compensated, lived on a golf course, and drove a new white Mercedes. I strived to be spiritual and financially successful in my business. I tried to keep my materialism quiet, played down my financial success (other than the splashy new car), and continued as a church elder living the moral and righteous life to balance it all out. Mine was not a fully honest and transparent life, of course, but I was doing the best I could at the time. Being gay was a condemnation that forced me to hide, and sometimes lie, for my own protection and self-preservation. Interestingly, the same JW folks who quietly whispered behind my back about my Mercedes started coming to me in private and asking for financial help.

"Can you lend me money for a new car at a lower rate than the bank?" one fellow congregation member asked me. *Now wait a minute*, I thought. I was not Dan Bolen First National Bank of Boise. I tactfully steered clear of these financial entanglements. There were times when the requests were nominal amounts, such as a few hundred dollars to help with bills, emergency dental visits, car repairs, or other surprise expenses. In many of those instances I just gave the money away as a gift without any expectations, which fed my own ego and people-pleasing orientation more than anything: *Wow, that Dan Bolen is a great guy! So successful, so generous, so decent. No wonder he's an elder.*

I also continued pioneering. One particular morning in Meridian, we were met at the door by a man who had a pistol in his hand.

"Get off my property!" He lived in a mobile home park.

"No problem, I'm outta here," I said as we backed out through the gate.

The brother who was pioneering with me had been a weightlifting trainer for Olympic athletes in the forties. As I was backpedaling, my church brother was still standing there trying to reason with this guy waving a gun. This scared the jeepers out of me!

DEAN and I were both living the American dream—hard-working types from meager small-town beginnings who had become financially successful, morally upright (both JWs), and model family men. In both our cases, though, that last category was more shiny veneer than truth; both our home lives were already unraveling, for different reasons. For me, because I was always either working, preparing for a JW teaching, preaching or teaching the good news, or at the congregation, I missed a lot of what was happening at home.

Eileen's drinking had escalated. Tiffany would come home from school and find her mom sleeping off the effects of too much Gallo wine. Along with the day drinking, Eileen had developed an unhealthy enmeshment with our daughter, an entanglement I missed because I was always out of the house. It would get so severe that they would team up against me when I tried to set boundaries. Eileen was a compulsive eater, too, whose health declined as she gained more than one hundred pounds. This greatly diminished my sexual attraction to my wife, who had once wowed me with her sultry strut in the white go-go boots. When we first met, Eileen was beautiful in every way, outgoing, and funny. I figured out later I was initially drawn to her not because she was a knockout, but rather because I sensed innately that she was someone who would give me a never-ending parade of issues to unravel and "fix." Dan Bolen, the professional people-pleaser and fixer, needed a long list of projects to fill a self-esteem tank that was never much above empty.

Rather than confronting my wife and offering to get her real help, my ego told me I could fix her problems myself. I was, after all, good at keeping secrets per the rule book (Dad's abuse, Mom's new religion, and my sexuality, to name a few). I was also a respected church elder who didn't want any embarrassment. Better to just pretend everything was great, keep working, keep preaching, and keep fixing problems on my own.

As my wife struggled with her weight, I started becoming critical of anyone who was overweight and obese, an issue I still have not resolved fully. My judgment was always immediate, even before meeting someone. I was embarrassed to admit this, because I wanted others to accept me as a gay man, and, yet, I was not accepting of others who were overweight. And overweight people could always lose weight; I'd never lose the gay. I could not yet understand that my recrimination of obese people was self-judgment and an inability to accept myself as gay. Instead, it was easier to obsessively monitor my own weight every day, lest I become obese myself.

I believe God has a good sense of humor, because He led me to marry two women who were both in great shape when we met, and then in both marriages my wives struggled with being overweight. I even made my second wife, Sandy, (we'll get to her) promise me she would not become obese, a twisted sort of verbal prenuptial agreement containing an obesity clause. She made the promise, and then apologized when she broke the promise. Meanwhile, I never told her before we got married that she was marrying a gay man. Ah… the twisted web I'd woven.

BACK to the go-getter eighties: From the outside, the Bolen brothers, Dan and Dean, could do no wrong. And we wore the badge of our workplace success proudly.

Every year the executive leadership of Management Recruiters put on a glitzy and expensive celebration to honor the top performers. The top three running the company were Alan Schoenberg, president and CEO; Lou Scott, vice president; and Bob Anderson, the director of franchises I had met on my first trip to Cleveland, who doubted Boise, Idaho, was a viable outpost. Each year they'd pick an exotic palm-treed locale, such as the Bahamas, Hawaii, Puerto Rico, or Mexico, rent out a block of rooms at a big resort, and send hundreds of us and our spouses to be showered with praise. For five days we relaxed, played golf, had business meetings, schmoozed at endless cocktail parties, and boozed during, between, and after all those activities. On one of those trips, Bob Anderson interviewed me on camera about how my firm in small-town U.S.A. was producing such gaudy numbers. His goal was to replicate my success in other small markets by using the video that included my secrets to success. The capper of the entire trip was the big gala, something akin to the Academy Awards for professional recruiting. None of us knew who the winners were until they were announced at the event. At the big event in 1979, my younger brother and employee Dean was called up on stage.

"Ladies and gentlemen, the number one national recruiter of the year is… Dean Bolen, of Management Recruiters of Boise." That meant he was first among all the recruiters working at more than 600 offices across the country.

I was honored to join him on stage that night as working manager of the year, which meant I was the number one producing manager among 600 offices (I won this award a second time, as well as national manager of the year, a run of three such awards never matched by anyone in the history of the company). Management Recruiters, it turned out, became another family for me, where I was showered with the public accolades and affirmation I craved but never got from my family of origin, and never received as publicly from my JW family.

I couldn't have been prouder of what we had accomplished, and experiencing a standing ovation together under the lights would be the highlight of our relationship as brothers. Dean was on stage that night because he had followed my directions after I'd promised him I would teach him everything he needed to know to become successful. Well, at least how to become successful in the recruiting business. There was a much bigger success—in living honestly in one's own truth and creating happy and healthy human relationships—that would elude us both. Dean would never get there, and I would only find my true success and transparency decades later, at age 70. But back in the early eighties it was all about piling up the work wins, taking home the awards, and vowing to go bigger in the coming year.

No one had private offices, including me, because it was important to have everything out in the open. That way I could hear the phones ringing, listen in on sales calls, and offer in-the-moment coaching. I had the ability to be on my own marketing call and listen to my people at the same time.

"Would you mind if I placed you on a brief hold?" I'd say. Then I'd turn to one of my employees and whisper, "Dean, don't say that! Back to the basics: feel, felt, found."

I remember one day hearing an enormous clatter coming from Dean's cubicle. When I ran over, he was sitting there staring at a completely empty desk. Everything, including his phone, paperwork, desk blotter, and the rest was piled up on the floor on one side of his desk.

"Danny, I'm just starting over right now."

I smiled. I always taught my people that we all had bad days. Whenever you caught yourself mired and spinning downward, you learned to hit reset and salvage whatever hours remained. Dean had simply hit reset in a dramatic and effective way!

Another tool I created was simple and effective; we called it the "FAB sheet," which incorporated my "features, accomplishments, and benefits" technique, eventually plagiarized throughout the recruiting business and still widely used in the industry today. We had each candidate list their features, accomplishments, and benefits as a way to present themselves well to a prospective employer. If a candidate was light on experience in a critical area, we had them steal any thunder by bringing it up first during the interview—like a skilled lawyer telling the jury the other side's strategy first. We had each candidate create their FAB sheet to match what the employer had told us were the key characteristics they were seeking in an employee. At the end of the interview, the candidate would hand the FAB sheet to the prospective employer. This worked so effectively because prospective employers typically remembered less than half of what the candidate said in an interview; the FAB sheet left the employer with one hundred percent of what was important to retain.

"Now, you'll see I only have one year of experience with centrifugal pumps. But more importantly, let me tell you what I accomplished in that year, which I think you'll find is really the equivalent of the five years you're seeking…"

As we prospered, I moved our branch of Management Recruiters to a larger office space at the upscale Park Center, where legendary brands Ore-Ida and Albertsons also had corporate offices. We started on the bottom floor and eventually moved to the top floor, with a beautiful view of the lake. There were six account executives including Dean, and our secretary Nova Newman. I was personally making $300,000 to $400,000 every year, which was big money in the early eighties. To multitask, I'd take Tiffany to the office on Saturdays, where she'd play on the typewriters. Sadly, in hindsight, every work success was matched by a failure at home.

Eileen repeatedly told me I needed to spend more time with our daughter, beyond just taking her to the office once a week, and she was right. There was one instance where Tiffany had baked and frosted a cake for a school cakewalk. I was supposed to pick her up at a specific time and take her to the event. Work consumed me, as it always did, and I showed up in my white Mercedes an hour late. The image of my 10-year-old daughter sitting on the curb with her cake makes my heart ache to this day. I'd crushed her, and for what exactly? Because I couldn't stop working, even when I was above and beyond everyone else in

Boise, the Western region, and across the entire country. No one called it "work addiction" in the eighties, but that's exactly what it was. One consequence is that I missed those important formative years when Tiffany was a pre-teen and then a teenager.

Concurrently, as Dean rose to the top of the ranks at work with my help, I didn't know he was already carrying even darker secrets than I. After my older brother, Lee, left home to join the Army and I was off to University of Alaska in Fairbanks, Dean was left as the only Bolen boy at home. Also still at home were Sue, Kay, Jo, and Marie.

During that time Dean unleashed his darkness on one of those sisters; I would only learn about this in the nineties, after he choked me. Then Dean left to attend Boise State University, which left the girls to fend for themselves as our father turned the emotional abuse on them. While our mother did not approve of her husband's behavior, she did very little to stop it or protect her children. That's why I still have an issue with Mom to this day; Dad was Dad, but Mom's offense was hard for me because she knew better and never stepped up. She believed staying with Dad despite the abuse was consistent with being in the JW church. Protecting the twin reputations—Bolen family and church—was more important than stopping what was really going on in the family. We all carefully maintained the secret of the perfect Bolen family, so that no one at the congregation ever found out what really went on in the household.

Once, after all the boys had left home, Dad got into yet another altercation with Mom; he took his gun out to the driveway, yelled that he was going to kill himself, and then went inside the motorhome and slammed the door. The next hour was agonizing as my mother and sisters cried hysterically and waited for the fateful shot to ring out. Gunfire never did crack the eerie silence. Instead, eventually Dad stumbled back inside holding the pistol, went to his room, and passed out for the night. I only know this because one of my sisters shared this story with me — so again, she kept the secret even from other family members.

AS I rose in my career, my personal life trended downward. In addition to drinking and overeating, Eileen started compulsively spending more and more money, along with raging. She practiced her deceit by hiding her spending from me with credit card account bills sent to secret post office boxes I didn't know about, and I practiced mine by hiding my true self from her. With mutual deceit as our foundation, she stayed home and indulged in all her patterns while I left the house to indulge in mine: work, religion, and exercise (yes, that, too, starting with racquetball, running, and weightlifting). In Bolen World, everything was a compulsion, nothing ever in moderation. William Shakespeare captured perfectly in *The Merchant of Venice* what Dean and I were each living in different ways: "The sins of the father are to be laid upon the children."

Twelve

Our World Could Not Function Without Rotating Machinery

I ALWAYS THOUGHT I HAD TO HAVE ALL THE answers. In my family of origin, I was financially successful and had become the appointed Fix-It Guy. *Go ask Danny; he'll know what to do, and he has money.* At work, since I was the owner and manager. *Go ask Dan; he's number one in the country.* At the congregation, since I was an elder. *Go talk to Dan Bolen; he's a great guy and an elder.* And at home, since I was the father. *Go ask your dad; he'll know.*

It was exhausting having everyone expecting me to know all the answers, all the time. But it also fed right into my people-pleasing, because I could give everyone what they wanted, namely answers, ideas, solutions, money, or whatever else would fix the problem—i.e., make me the hero. That's why any form of even well-meaning constructive criticism was difficult for me to accept, because, after all, I was always the guy who had the answers. How could anyone criticize Dan Bolen for anything? Dan Bolen knew everything! All of it fed into supporting my ego.

I was a perfectionist, too—so there was no room for anyone to criticize me, because I did everything "perfectly." Number one at work. Number one at the congregation as an elder. Number one at fitness. And number one, at least in appearance, as a husband and father with a happy marriage, a happy home life, and a house on a golf course. I craved external validation, for others to tell me how much they liked me because I couldn't like myself… the dark secret I had buried worked its toxic decay under the cover of my denial. At work, however, I was somebody, because I was so passionate about what I did. Passion led to success beyond my wildest dreams. And success led to validation, a diluted external back-slap that never filled me with the true self-esteem I craved.

"This is a dead deal," I said, sitting in a Management Recruiters office in Milwaukee. "It ain't happening." I had been secretly listening to this young male account executive's call using a suction cup on the phone without the other party's knowledge or consent. It was 1985, so no one ever asked if we could legally listen in on and record calls. The only thing that mattered was production. I'd been hired, at a nice fee, by the owner of this franchise to turn his losing operation around by asking tough questions and boosting production.

"Pick up the phone and call this prospect instead," I said.

The young man just stared at me, unable to let go of the candidate I could clearly see was someone on the road to nowhere. The recruiters all knew who I was, by reputation. Many who worked there were eager for my help; others, like this young man, were scared I was there to push them out of their job, which was not my intention.

"Now please pick up the phone, because we're moving on. I want you to be the best you're capable of being. You're better than this, and I'm going to push you to be your best. Now let's go: We're making twenty more calls before we leave here today."

He glanced at the clock: it was 3:40 p.m. He probably hadn't ever made twenty calls in an entire day. "Twenty more?"

"Yes, you are correct, twenty more! I know you're capable of doing it, so let's go! I'll be here with you to help you get there."

I thought he might cry, but instead he picked up the receiver and dialed (yes, Spin of the Dial) the first of twenty new calls that we did indeed complete by just after 6 p.m. Within ninety days of my up-close-and-personal tough love in Milwaukee, production volume at that Management Recruiters office went up 100 percent. The people-pleaser Dan Bolen had swooped in and singlehandedly doubled their production. The adrenaline rush of such accomplishments kept me buzzing for weeks.

The year 1985 was a transitional time, because I had told my executive leadership team that I was leaving Management Recruiters to start my own recruiting firm—a firm that was not going to be part of their organization, which was the franchise I owned in Boise. My new operation was going to be named, simply and aptly, Dan Bolen and Associates.

Being so successful under the MR banner, how had I come to such a potentially risky decision? First, I was the number-one producer across more than 600 offices and had no more mountains to climb at Management Recruiters; I needed a new and bigger challenge. Eileen, too, had tired of Boise—the long winters, the cold and soggy spring (mud) season—and she needed a change of scenery. She was struggling with various health issues, too, and wanted to go back to California where she had gone to high school. I was certainly amenable to the idea of steady sunshine, after only ever living in predominantly cold, gray states: Alaska, Idaho, and Washington.

Another factor: I was paying Management Recruiters a seven percent franchise fee, so on every $100,000 our office generated, $7,000 came off the top. If I could produce at the same level on my own—say, $1,000,000 annually—there was an extra $70,000 I'd get to keep, without any additional work.

Also, I had an idea to really specialize my focus; after filling a number of positions in the rotating machinery industry, I had learned that the planet could not function without rotating machinery (more on that later). Dan Bolen and Associates would be solely operating in the industries that designed, manufactured, installed, sold, and serviced pumps, compressors, turbines, and, later, valves.

My new number-one producer at Management Recruiters was Craig Alexander, who was interested in buying the franchise. Craig moved to the top when Dean left to start his own firm, which had been fine by me. Dean divorced and moved to Arizona to start over. However, he also took one of my other top producers with him, which had not been fine by me. This was the first big crack in the foundation of my relationship with my younger brother, which would finally crumble completely the night he choked me at his daughter's wedding.

Craig and I struck a deal for a ten-year buyout, including my pledge that I would not directly compete by taking his clients and candidates. Craig owned that Management Recruiters franchise in Boise that I had established until 2021 when he sold the company. Of course, when I told the Management Recruiters brass their number-one golden goose was flying away, they were beyond distraught. They tried to change my mind with lavish offers, but my decision had been made. It was time for me to strike out with my new company, under my own name, with no limitations on my success. When they realized the bird had already left the cage, they suggested the next-best thing, which was for me to do a series of seminars. If they couldn't keep Dan Bolen, at least they could harness some of the keys to my success. I had already done two videos for the company, and I loved the idea of sharing everything I knew. Of course I did: that was People-Pleasing 101.

Dan Bolen and Associates began operations from our house on the golf course in the Eagle Hills suburb in 1985. I was a solo operator. Concurrently, my arrangement with Management Recruiters was $5,000 for my one-day seminar and $10,000 for the two-day version. Over the next couple years I did about fifteen of these seminars across the country, from New York City to Los Angeles and stops in between, even including some international seminars. This required increasing my work hours from the standard seventy hours a week to eighty and sometimes ninety hours a week, not including the time I was spending on church activities. Talk about work addiction and religion addiction.

When I wasn't traveling for Management Recruiters, I spent my days sourcing candidates who were experts at rotating machinery: turbines, pumps, and compressors. I also marketed my outstanding candidates to new companies. Interestingly, I had no technical ability of my own, and I didn't even like mechanical things. But I knew how to find the best people and put them in the jobs they wanted, at good companies. I knew my clients' competitors better than they did, and I was richly rewarded financially. Along with my seminar fees, my income soared to as much as $200,000 in a single month—although the next month I might be "down" to $50,000.

I had it all, at least career-wise. And when I was in the ministry preaching, people could see and feel my deep, caring love for them. That was no act, and was the genuine core of who I was. And yet, I could not give myself the same grace and self-love. I could not enjoy the honest success of just being real. And, at the time, I believed I could not talk about my incongruence with my family, friends, or anyone in the church—because all the parts of my world were built on denial of who I was as a gay man. This denial led to me suffer severe depression, which started in 1984 and continued into 1985. Even as I was earning more money every month than many people earned in an entire year, my depression worsened after I'd started my own company. I would lie on the floor, alone, and sob and sob for an hour or more, not knowing that I was clinically depressed. I'd collapse into bed late at night and then wake up completely depressed again. Just getting out of bed and combing my hair was a chore. Many of the

Bolen children struggled with depression at one time or another. For me, the idea of suicide became a constant and comforting companion: If the pain became unbearable I could always go to sleep... forever. When I was in the grasp of that severe pain, one way I found temporary relief was working out at the gym. Another was proselytizing in the field ministry and attending meetings in the congregation. And the other was working; I could always pull myself together to perform at work.

Asking for help was not an option, because I believed I had to keep everything perfect so no one ever saw any of my flaws. I could not fail: admitting or showing my depression to anyone would be failure. I told myself that while my wife may have been drinking way too much, she was not an alcoholic—because assigning that label would mean I had failed as a husband.

There were many days where that final escape hatch seemed to be the only way out of the dark pain. I lived on a knife's edge of contemplating suicide for several years. Voltaire said it best: "The man who, in a fit of melancholy, kills himself today, would have wished to live had he waited a week."

I thank God, my lucky stars, and every other helpful talisman that I instead chose to wait—*not today*—and take one trudging step forward by getting off the office floor, blowing my nose, taking a few deep breaths, climbing back onto my chair, and starting to make calls again.

When you're off the phone, you're unemployed. Or dead.

When a candidate or employer asked me why my voice had changed, I just said I was battling a cold. I finally sought out a Boise psychiatrist, who agreed to see me immediately on a weekend because I wasn't sure I was going to make it to Monday. He diagnosed me with severe depression, prescribed medication, and sent me back into the trenches. I kept that visit a secret from everyone, including my wife and daughter. In late 1985, we moved south to the sunbelt and landed in California, first in Rancho Mirage and then Indian Wells, where we bought a home. Despite the sunny new surroundings, I was still battling my demons, trying to hold back the suicidal thoughts, and denying who I was. My only solution was to just get back on the phone and get connected to the new congregation in Palm Desert.

It was a sad way to live.

Thirteen

Like Ugly on an Ape

IN 1996, MY DIVORCE FROM THE BEAUTIFUL GIRL in the white go-go boots was final. I was so ashamed and felt like a complete failure. Over the previous decades I had given everything to God and the Jehovah's Witness organization: my college education, my commitment, my time, my entire being, my life. Then, when I most needed support, they offered no comfort—because mine was not a scriptural divorce. Let me explain this rule.

As a JW, only verified adultery authorized a scriptural divorce, which happened one of two ways. One way was bringing forth at least two witnesses willing to testify about the alleged heinous act. The other was a full admission by one of the partners that they committed adultery. I had neither of those. However, I would need one of those solutions if I would ever be allowed to remarry. And because mine was not authorized as scriptural, the JW rules were clear: I was not allowed to marry again.

As of the date of my divorce, I could not remarry or date (because the only reason to date was future marriage, which I was barred from pursuing), have sex (because I was out of wedlock and also not permitted to enter wedlock), or masturbate (just for good measure; I'd only done this three times in the prior eighteen years). If someone from the congregation so much as saw me holding a girl's hand (or, Good Lord, a boy's!), they'd be on me like a hungry dog on a bone. So for the next eighteen years I would not be allowed to date or be alone with a woman. I stayed faithful to that pledge for eighteen years as a single man who could never marry again.

How did I do this? And why? Was I brain dead? No, I was not. Most importantly, when I had joined this new family and gotten baptized, we were brothers and sisters to each other. I was Brother Bolen and treated kindly. There was genuine love and concern expressed among us. As I'd learned as a child, I followed the rules set down by my dad. To keep your family, you followed the rules, even the rules that were unfair. The pain of losing this new family, even as draconian as it became, was still a greater pain than whatever I had to suffer. This emotional hold to stay in my chosen family, at whatever cost to myself, defied any logic.

Looking back, I'm ashamed and embarrassed. But at the time, I'm not sure I could have done things any differently based on the family of origin I'd survived.

THE meteoric upswing in my professional career, as the sole proprietor of Dan Bolen and Associates from 1985 to the midnineties, tracked with my greatest personal downfall, which was being unable to save my marriage. Despite all my best attempts, denials, and two expensive inpatient treatments for my wife Eileen (more on that in a moment), I had failed. Eileen and I were married twenty-six years. The early years were wonderful; the last ten years were hell. At work I was an industry whiz kid, the one-man dynamo of the rotating machinery world who had successfully gone solo in recruiting, something most people in the field simply could not do. I was the motivator of others, and I led because I loved business and all the people I encountered daily on the phone and in person. Almost immediately from its formation, Dan Bolen and Associates became number one in rotating machinery placements. Talk about an unknown entity in an obscure industry; I was carving out a highly refined niche.

Work was my addiction, and a big part of that addiction was burying who I was, which kept me away from home, where I should have been, especially for my daughter. Sadly, Tiffany was an innocent caught between two adults trying to unravel their own intricate knots. I take responsibility for the big secret and the domino-effect issues I brought to the marriage.

By the end, young love had been replaced by Eileen being lost in a thicket of her deceit, anger, physical abuse, rage, addictions, drinking, and compulsive spending. I, too, added to the mix in different ways with my work and constant proselytizing. By the time we brought in the lawyers, all that was left was sorting through the rubble and determining who got what. I retained a savvy attorney who wanted to make sure I didn't have to go head-to-head with a former judge turned divorce attorney who, by reputation, was a bare-knuckle brawler who would ruthlessly drag me through years of painful legal maneuvers, procedures, and increasing demands. At my attorney's behest, I made an appointment with that same ruthless lawyer and paid him the initial $220 fee to discuss my impending divorce. That single meeting was a deft sleight of hand, because it established attorney-client privilege with me and forbid him from representing Eileen as her attorney in our divorce. I was saddened that a union that had started with the highest intentions and produced a beautiful daughter had been reduced to such exacting legal tactical maneuvers. But I felt I had no choice, because things had really gone haywire in those last years.

AS I mentioned, the late eighties were a dark time for me as I battled severe depression. Suicidal thoughts became a friend to me. Sleep was my only release. And the mantra I repeated was, *if things get any worse I can just go to sleep.* At the deep core of my struggle was the fact that I was hiding who I was. It was easier to casually contemplate suicide than to admit, even to myself, that I was a gay man. That was the insanity I brought to my marriage, a deep denial that cast a heavy shadow in our household and on my wife.

For twelve years while we lived in California, I was the Theocratic Ministry School overseer at the Palm Desert Congregation of Jehovah's Witnesses, another title, list of duties, and addiction to keep me from facing my reality and my home life. I liked being at the congregation where I was surrounded by yet more Dan Bolen admirers, nice people who lived by good standards. They formed the family I never had. That's why I was a devout JW for so long. In hindsight, in following "the truth" I was blind to the actual truth: these "nice" people would have quickly cast me out if I ever acted on my secret identity.

And sure, there were certain organizational principles that were difficult to square. But again, I never stepped out of line to challenge or go against any dogma, because the reward I enjoyed, namely familial love (however conditional, tainted, and twisted it might have been), was too great. So I buried all my objections along with my sexuality, and went back to work. I still believe in God. I believe in Jesus. I even still support many of the benevolent JW teachings. However, I no longer support all the organizational rules, which are too unrealistic. A 19-year-old kid who can't have sex until he or she gets married needs to be able to masturbate. Yes, it is a human *need*. Look no further than the Catholic Church to see how demanding total abstinence has worked out.

And I also don't believe in all the hypocrisy and secrecy when those who proclaim to be righteous in the JW faith are in actuality just flawed people working around the system to image-manage. In the early nineties I was still one of the smoke-and-mirror faithful, an imperfect human being casting a projection of perfection. But I was certainly not alone in practicing my parlor tricks. Demanding perfection from imperfect human beings creates a culture of denial, deceit, and dishonesty, which all go against the stated goal of the supposedly righteous. Still, in the early nineties I was all in as a proud JW.

I also made sure I never had time to cross paths with my actual self. On the nights I wasn't teaching at the congregation, I would work until 9 p.m. to avoid going home. In Indian Wells, I ran my business out of a rented office at an executive-suite facility that included a common secretary. I was completely absorbed at work, which kept the real Dan Bolen buried. Meanwhile, to kill all those idle hours during the day and into the evening, my wife had discovered a relatively new cable TV offering, the Home Shopping Network, and later QVC, which was launched in 1986: quality, value, and convenience. My personal experience would be that those three words would cost us to the tune of tens of thousands of dollars.

Thanks to QVC, Eileen could enjoy twin indulgences—wine and shopping—without ever leaving home. She had televisions sets on throughout the house and would make numerous purchases throughout the day. And because I was always gone, it was easy for her to meet the delivery drivers at the front door and hide everything long before I came home. Our closet filled up with new clothes, still with their tags on, in smaller sizes for when Eileen's weight came off. We owned six identical duffel bags we would never use. She had jewelry she never wore, and makeup she never used. I first caught a glimpse of this secret life when I found a receipt she had forgotten to put away. Thankfully for me, there was no receipt for my homosexuality for anyone to find on the kitchen counter.

"This credit card number doesn't match any of ours."

"You don't give me enough money," she said.

Those two statements highlighted the gulf between our two positions in what became a long night of protracted negotiation. In the end she came clean, apologized profusely, and admitted she had opened two credit card accounts with a combined balance of around $10,000. To cover her tracks, she had the statements sent to a secret box she had opened at the post office.

"I'm so sorry," she said repeatedly.

It was a big shock to me, and an unexpected financial hit, but not a death blow because I was doing well. I demanded that we close the accounts. Then I wrote checks to pay off what I thought was the total of our outstanding credit card debt.

"It will never happen again," she said again. "I'm so sorry."

"Are these the only ones?"

"Yes."

"You don't owe any more?"

"No."

I believe my wife's intention was pure when she said those things. However, in hindsight, it would have been like me vowing to never sneak another glance at a naked man in the health club locker room: a well-intentioned promise I would never be able to keep.

"It will never happen again," I might have said. "I'm so sorry."

"Was he the only one?"

"Yes."

"You won't look at anyone else?"

"No."

With that context, it wasn't long before we repeated the cycle for a second time: more credit card accounts discovered, with secret P.O. box numbers, and thousands more in debt that I paid off. Eileen made her promises again, and I went back to work with this horrible feeling in my gut that she was going to bankrupt us. It made me physically ill.

My wife's compulsions played out more openly, where I could challenge her and righteously demand she stop. Less drinking. Less spending. Concurrently, my work and church compulsions were not only socially acceptable, they were lauded by all.

How does Brother Bolen do it all? So successful and so giving of his time at the congregation.

In the theater of war that our marriage had become, it was an unfair fight for sure. And when you went to war, there was never a winner. Only more pain, carnage, and casualties.

Fourteen

The Way of Truth

DR. JERRY MEYER DIRECTED ME TO THE BASEMENT. I stood outside the door, my heart racing, peering through the smudged window at a group of men and women seated in a circle of metal folding chairs. The setting looked exactly as I'd seen on TV shows and in films, the bare metal table with white foam cups and a pot of coffee brewing. The block walls painted white and dotted with crooked posters.

But for the grace of God, there go I.
Easy does it.
First things first.

I was like an explorer peeking through jungle foliage at a culture and community I'd never glimpsed. The strange Zen riddles only heightened my confusion, because this felt anything but easy, and I had no clue what first thing was supposed to come first. And had God led me there? To keep me from going where?

The Al Anon meeting began, and I remained at my post

outside the room in the basement of the hospital in Palm Desert. Although there were three empty chairs, I could not muster whatever I was lacking to enter that room. Then I read another poster.

Al Anon members are people, just like you, who are worried about someone with a drinking problem.

That one, at least, hit the mark. I was worried about someone with a drinking problem. Except the other problem was that Eileen would not attend Alcoholics Anonymous, even at the behest of our therapist Dr. Meyer. He had suggested I go to this Al Anon meeting at the hospital. I was almost at the meeting... except I knew if I walked through the doorway I would have to admit my wife was an alcoholic. I turned and went home instead.

Mahatma Gandhi said, "The way of truth and love have always won." Eileen's truth came out as our marriage unraveled in the late eighties and early nineties. My deepest truth would remain buried for almost three more decades. However, as Eileen's truth came out, it forced me to start chiseling at my own thick wall of denial. Two weeks after I'd first tried, I was back in the basement, standing outside the room again, trying to find the courage. A woman about my age, who looked like an executive in her crisp blue skirt and jacket with a white silk blouse, smiled at me.

"Welcome. I'm Trudy."

"Hi. I'm Dan."

We shook hands and both stood there.

"First time?"

I nodded. She nodded. "It works if you work it. And you're worth it."

As a savvy trained salesman, I admired her pitch because it was so unexpected, just direct and disarming. And genuine. Trudy was selling a product she believed in, a set of World Book encyclopedias for the soul. I had the odd sensation of being transported back to my college dorm room, with Bruce Benson leaning against the door jamb and spooling out his disarming questions.

Do you know it is impossible for God to lie?

Dr. Meyer had told me that when the student was ready, the teacher would appear. Bruce had been my teacher. And now here was Trudy, a complete stranger, communicating the same things without saying anything: *I understand how you feel. I know a lot of people, including myself, felt the same thing before. And what I've found is…*

Despite still being terrified, I nodded at Trudy, held the door open for her, and then followed her into the room. I would attend Al Anon meetings in that basement for the next five years. However, for the first three meetings I never spoke beyond introducing myself.

"Hi. I'm Dan."

"Hi, Dan," everyone said in unison.

"I'm just going to listen, thanks."

"Thanks, Dan."

During my fourth meeting, after introducing myself I dipped my toe in the waters: "I really relate to each of you and the stories you're sharing. I'm working on some things in my marriage, too. Thank you."

"Thanks, Dan."

At my fifth meeting, I took the first brick out of the wall: "My name is Dan, and my wife is an alcoholic."

"Hi, Dan."

Oh my God, what had I done! I'd publicly admitted failure, my glaring failure. My wife's drinking was just like my dad's, a pain I'd vowed to never go through again. I'd never talked to anyone at the church about Eileen, because I didn't want my position as an elder to be in jeopardy. More so, I feared my self-image and ego were about to take a big hit because I had a wife who was an alcoholic, an embarrassment I could not fathom. Except I was admitting my failure in public, to a group of strangers. Well-meaning strangers, yes, but I didn't know these people from Adam! I quickly scanned the circle to make sure no one from the congregation was there.

I did not feel any relief, just shame and embarrassment. And that, I would discover, was the beauty of that basement: unlike at the congregation, I did not feel judged. There I was admitting dark truths— my wife was an alcoholic—and people just nodded knowingly, thanked me, and hugged me afterward. Al Anon saved me. I walked into that basement believing I was going to learn slick new strategies on how to control Eileen's drinking. Al Anon gave me a completely different set of tools called the three C's: I did not Cause anyone's behavior, I could never Control anyone's behavior, and I could never Cure anyone's behavior.

I went to two or three meetings a week. Initially, Eileen didn't even know I was going. The student was finally ready, and Al Anon was my teacher. I had become obsessed with her drinking, but hadn't done anything to help myself. When I thought I was in control of her alcoholism, her disease was just outside doing pushups. I talked about things in that group I'd never mentioned with anyone at work or church. For the first time in my life I took off my mask for the hour I was in that basement.

When I admit she's an alcoholic, I feel like a failure.
I work because I don't want to go home.

I identified my work as an addiction for the first time, a cross-addiction with my wife's drinking and spending. The biggest relief I found in that basement was realizing my story, struggle, and pain were not unique. I had been so wrapped up in my career, trying to save my marriage, and devoting myself to the congregation that I never stopped to think about who Dan Bolen really was.

When Eileen learned I was going to Al Anon she said, "I'm not an alcoholic." This was where the rubber met the road: how would I react to more crazymaking? I responded like a seasoned recovery pro: "I'm going to my Al Anon meetings for me, not you. I have a problem, which is how I react to your choices."

Of course, while I'd partially removed my mask, there were places I still could not go under any circumstances. In the early nineties, even among the full support of my Al Anon group whom

I considered trusted friends, I would have committed suicide before admitting I was gay.

ALTHOUGH my Al Anon meetings helped me understand the disease of alcoholism and learn to focus on myself, things would definitely get worse before they got better. When our therapist diagnosed Eileen with Borderline Personality Disorder, she responded, "Dan's borderline, not me." That statement, of course, shows exactly what people who are borderline do: project their issues onto others. Al Anon taught me to accept what I could not change, and I could not change Eileen's thinking or behavior. But eventually, the drinking and episodes of screaming and rage from her led to Eileen agreeing to go to an inpatient treatment center. Her screaming and hitting me a number of different times while in the car had escalated severely. One time when I was driving her car to get it repaired, she went into a fit and started screaming and hitting me. I stopped and got out of the car, and she ran over my foot and left me standing there. Once while in Hawaii she started screaming, raging, and hitting me while I was driving on the freeway. She threw herself in the backseat, still kicking me with her legs and thrashing me in the back of my head, which almost caused a crash. I would just freeze and hang onto the steering wheel in hopes she would stop. Unfortunately, I didn't know what to do, and so I did nothing except retreat within myself and withdraw from her.

In 1992, Eileen went to the Betty Ford Center, in Rancho Mirage, California, for a thirty-day program that cost us $60,000. She raged at me for days, screaming various abuses, but finally agreed to go. I was relieved that for those thirty days she wouldn't be drinking or spending. If she was raging, it would be directed at therapists rather than me. Much later, I would realize I had chosen for a wife someone just like my father—an alcoholic, a rager, and someone who used distance (emotional and physical) to separate us. Eileen did get somewhat pensive, too, so I thought perhaps she was "sick and tired of being sick and tired," an old recovery slogan I'd heard many times at my meetings. Everyone who finally showed up at Al Anon was sick and tired for sure.

After the treatment, things got marginally better, but I'm not sure Eileen ever stopped drinking, and the compulsive spending continued. She was also hiding the amount of prescription medications she was using (Vicodin and Darvocet), which had doubled each year for three years in a row. She was supposed to go to ninety meetings in ninety days, but she did not while claiming she had. When I asked her about whether she was going to her meetings she would get extremely angry and yell, "That's none of your business; that's my recovery!"

Meanwhile, I joined a second group for men that was an offshoot of the Betty Ford program. We were all men with alcoholic wives. It was as part of that group that I used a small bat to beat the holy hell out of a pillow as I released so much hatred for my dad and how he had treated me. I cried hysterically and started the forgiveness process. I continued at Al Anon, too.

Then in 1994 everything at home exploded in a final culmination: another confrontation with another found receipt, a physical altercation during which Eileen came at me, and police involvement. This was the saddest day of my life, and it came four days before a Barbra Streisand concert for which we already had two tickets. I knew as the police officers tried to sort things out that my marriage was over. I was exhausted. I was done. That's the day we officially separated.

I called the church elders, told them what had happened to Brother Bolen, and went to Embassy Suites to get a room. A few days later I got an apartment at Palm Desert Club and hired attorney Larry Moore, who directed me to meet with the hardline attorney to void him from being involved in our divorce. Four days after the big blowup, Eileen and I still went to see Barbra Streisand, sat side by side in our pricey seats, and barely spoke. It was a heartbreaking day for both of us. The woman I'd married had a beautiful voice and had sung many Barbra Streisand songs to me over the years. We had each waited years for the chance to finally see Barbra perform live, but by the time the concert came, our marriage was done.

For two more years I attempted to salvage my marriage. Eileen was living in our house; I lived in the apartment and paid the mortgage on the house. Eileen also had a car I paid for, and she was getting $3,000 a month for other expenses. It was Eileen who officially instigated the divorce proceedings. Despite the improbability of things ever improving, I had held out hope until the bitter end. I went to my men's group at Betty Ford and through tears said that my marriage was over. I had officially failed, and had a tremendous amount of shame. One of my friends put his arm around me as I sat on the curb, still crying.

"It'll get better," he said. "Promise."

Despite the immense pain, there was the slightest glimmer of relief. But I was so exhausted by it all. I vowed to never get married again, because I could not envision ever trusting another woman. It was a domino effect from there, as my fellow elders strongly suggested I step down from my role. It was unspoken but clear: resign or be removed. I was so emotionally and mentally drained that a part of me felt relief giving up being an elder and all the church duties, which required a lot of preparation time. Besides, that would free up more time to work.

WE made a second expensive and final attempt to get Eileen help with another thirty-day inpatient treatment at The Meadows in Wickenburg, Arizona, to address her compulsive spending and addictive rage. Two weeks into the program Eileen said she wanted to leave. When I went to pick her up, she walked out of the facility carrying a box of new books.

"Where did you get those?" I asked.

"The gift shop."

"How?"

"Put them on my credit card."

I was angry as hell because she went there for spending addiction, and they allowed her to use her credit card in the gift shop. That was like going to Betty Ford Center for alcoholism and finding a bar set up in the lobby. Eileen left halfway through the treatment and flew to Hawaii where she could freely spend money. When the doctors at the Meadows realized what had happened, and how upset I was, they offered to allow Eileen back at no additional charge. However, that ship had sailed: Eileen refused to go back, because she said they were abusive to her.

Eileen gave me two great gifts: my daughter Tiffany and our divorce. Although I could not see it then, the divorce turned out to be a tremendous gift. What I've learned since: even with the worst tragedies, there is always a gift. It may not come immediately (and usually doesn't), but with acceptance and patience, it will arrive.

We sorted out the final terms in 1996. In reality, whatever debts I'd paid off were only the cold tip of a massive iceberg I would only fully discover at the end, when the lawyers were involved and we were both being deposed by the other side. The final forensic accounting: Eileen still had twenty-seven credit accounts, most maxed out, with all the statements going to secret post-office boxes. In the final eleven months of our marriage, when we were separated, she had racked up additional tens and tens of thousands in charges, including the new box of books from her treatment program.

Because of the nature of spending addiction, which lights up the pleasure centers in the brain similarly to sexual activity (and similarly to my trusty work addiction), I knew I needed to make a clean break, or I would have the financial sword of Damocles dangling above my head, forever suspended by only a single strand of horsehair. I told my attorney to tell Eileen's attorney I was giving her most of the money we had. All I was keeping was our house, which had a mortgage, and an IRA with several hundred thousand dollars. Eileen agreed and signed on the dotted line, which meant I'd never have to pay alimony or anything else ever. It was a clean excision, for me, of the voracious financial addictions I had been battling for more than a decade. If I had stayed in the marriage, over time she would have bankrupted us. My attorney said if I'd entered into an alimony arrangement it would be like having garlic around my neck for the rest of my life, a foul stench I'd never escape. The clean break brought me true relief.

I would have to start from scratch again on every front in my life. I had to admit I had failed. And since I'd never failed at anything in my life, this was an agonizing admission. I'd also had to step down as an elder, which meant I'd failed my flock and greatly disappointed my adopted family. The JW thread back to Bruce Benson was still intact, but I no longer had the ego boost of being an elder. I was now a "publisher," with fewer responsibilities in the JW faith. In my personal life, as a JW I could never remarry, have sex, or masturbate. To cling to my chosen family, I accepted these terms and vowed to live as a celibate man. And yet, at the health club I still stole quick glimpses of naked men in the locker room.

After the divorce was final in 1996 I moved to Arizona, where my sister Jo lived with her husband. I needed a clean break from California and any proximity to the life that had unraveled. I rented a two-bedroom condo at the San Antigua complex in Scottsdale, where I ran Dan Bolen and Associates out of one of the bedrooms. I retained my same secretary, who worked remotely out of the Palm Desert office suite.

This was the start of building a new life.

Fortuitously, the more pain I endured, the more money I made, because the love of my life was my job. And in 1996 I was untethered by any home life, marriage, parenting, or church elder duties. During that year of my divorce, Dan Bolen and Associates generated about $500,000. In the church basement and with my other men's group, I'd removed my mask and faced some truths for the first time in my life.

But I had no idea I'd still only scratched the surface. The full reckoning loomed, which would be much deeper and darker, but was still two decades away.

Fifteen

The Détente

BY THE END, DAD WAS TERRIFIED OF THE SNAKES he believed were slithering under his bed. He also saw ghastly bugs running up and down the walls.

"I'm so tired of these bugs on the wall," he said, clutching the bedspread to his neck.

"I think I got them all, Dad," I reassured him each time. At a family meeting, the staff where he lived had told us that it was better not to argue, or try to convince him that what he was seeing were illusions; better to just go along, soothe, and reassure him by "fixing" the problem. Mom still wanted to argue: *There are no bugs, Ben!*, which was never helpful. His dementia manifested in other ways, too. Earlier that morning, I'd borrowed his red Toyota truck to run errands and then saw, when I returned, that he was especially distraught.

"What's wrong, Dad?"

"I'm not happy with the way you treated my truck."

I glanced outside and nodded. "I'm so sorry. What did I do?"

"When you drove my pickup, you didn't unplug it," he said. "I can see the cord. You have to unplug it before you drive it." His truck was a nineties model, and this was 2010, long before electric vehicles were commonplace.

"Let me go check," I said, walking out with him following behind me while I got down on my hands and knees and carefully inspected under the truck. Then I mimicked what I thought might look like unplugging the imaginary cord. I nodded my approval at my work, in a long, exaggerated manner to make sure he saw.

"I am so sorry, Dad. You were right, but you saw that I made sure to unplug it."

My sisters Sue and Marie had already taken away his driver's license, which had unleashed a tremendous amount of outrage because that was one of the last freedoms Dad had at the end. Then we'd moved him into an assisted living facility in the 2000s, because his mental state had progressively worsened. The man we once feared and cowered before now relied on us for any connection back to a fading reality. Since they both lived in the Boise area, my sisters Sue and Marie had taken the helm in helping with his emotional and physical needs. I am so grateful they were there, and for the care and devotion they showed to our father. Meanwhile, when I traveled from Phoenix to visit, I was in charge of his financial affairs, pest control (snakes and bugs), and proper unplugging of imaginary cords. It had been an odd transition, a full decade in the making, as our relationship evolved from him as the father who I was convinced might accidentally — or intentionally — kill me, to finally standing up for myself… and then this final phase, the twilight of his life with his middle son as one of his caretakers.

THE détente had begun in 2000, in of all places, Apache Junction, Arizona, a dusty far-flung annex thirty-five miles east of Phoenix. In 1999, Mom and Dad had become snowbirds, splitting their time between Boise in the summer and Arizona for the winter. The Bolen contingent in Arizona included me as well, and would soon include my sisters Kay and Jo and their husbands. Having my father back in such close proximity for a chunk of each year coincided with the work I'd been doing on myself. I'd spent much of the nineties, as my first marriage unraveled, doing soul-searching in the hospital basement at my regular Al Anon meeting and at my men's support group through the Betty Ford Center. If the JW flock was the loving family I'd never had as a child, my two support groups were an extended family of loving, supportive, and caring people—the aunts, uncles, and cousins who just listened without judgment and reminded me I wasn't alone in any challenge I faced.

Through years of sharing and processing, I'd worked out a lot of my own rage against my father including beating a pillow with a small bat at my men's group and releasing old trauma through tears as my friends provided emotional support. Somewhere in that process, I also started forgiving my father for all his abuse, rage, and toxicity. Gradually, ever so slowly, I was able to see his truth: that he had been similarly abused by my grandfather. My new empathy did not excuse his behavior, but it helped depersonalize it. My father was stuck in a horrible, endless loop of anger—because that's what had been imprinted on him. Back to Shakespeare: "The sins of the father are to be laid upon the children." The cycle of abuse, from one father to his son, and from that son to his sons and daughters. Concurrently, I even started to see and appreciate the good things my dad had done for our family, for me, my mother, and my brothers and sisters. When you hate someone, you cannot see any good in them. Nothing. My difficult inner work started to rub away my father's grit to reveal the rough jewel that had always been there. Namely, he'd worked as much as humanly possible to provide for seven children.

By the time I moved to Scottsdale and, sadly, left those two support groups behind in California, my hatred of my father was slowly giving way to acceptance and forgiveness. With my new mindset and clarity, tolerating his bad ways was no longer possible. In my groups I'd learned about boundaries, which meant drawing lines around myself for self-protection. I'd decided it was no longer acceptable for Dad to come at me with the same toxic anger and rage he'd used to terrify me as a child. And because he was nearby in Arizona every winter, it was easy to set a lunch meeting for The Big Talk. Although my dad didn't know it, I'd called him to the eighties franchise holdover TGI Friday's to lay down the law, which was that I was not going to take his abuse anymore. Not ever again.

We started with potato skins as an appetizer and the usual small talk, which always centered around the ever-humming enterprise Dan Bolen and Associates. Dad's pride at my financial acumen and success in the business world gave us a comfortable shared topic that would have easily been a safe harbor through the entire meal and saying our goodbyes. However, I was not going to take the avoidance path again. Instead, as we took the last bites of our hamburgers and French fries, I broached the subject without any of the fear I might have anticipated.

"Dad, there's something I need to tell you." He nodded, but had no idea where this was headed. "I love you as my father, but I don't like the way you've treated me, my mother, and my siblings." Now that got his attention. I was 53 years old, and I'd never spoken to my father in such a real, unfiltered way about anything, let alone matters of the heart and soul. "Now, I can't set Mom's boundaries, but I can set mine. If you ever rage at me again, then we will no longer have a relationship. If you explode and attempt to take out your anger on me, I will be gone, and our relationship will be over. I will never, ever take any more abuse from you. Not verbally. Not physically. Not emotionally. Not ever. If any abuse ever happens again, even one time, I will have to separate myself from you."

What I was doing felt like the equivalent of lobbing a live

grenade into a fireworks warehouse, so I braced for the almost-certain blowback. But amazingly, instead of detonating a Krakatoa reaction that would get us both tossed out of the restaurant, my father did something I had never seen him do. He wept. His tears deepened the sense of empathy I'd already been mining on my own for years. From that moment forward, our relationship changed. I had successfully set a boundary that he would never violate. Of course, I had also done it without letting him know who the real Danny was, because that was a bridge I wasn't ready to cross.

A few months after the big summit, I went to Mom's and Dad's double-wide mobile home in Apache Junction, where they had a great view of Superstition Mountain. I took a Hallmark card I'd gotten him. Inside I'd written things that I'd never shared with my father, about how much I loved him, how grateful I was that he was in my life, and that I had forgiven him. He read it in the other room while I waited. He never said a word as he came out of the bedroom crying again and looked at me straight on. Through his tears I saw kindness in his eyes; it was only the second time I'd seen him cry, and the first time I had ever seen kindness.

Good Lord, who was this new man I'd unearthed?

He looked straight at me, and I sensed this was his way of telling me that he had in turn forgiven me for any perceived transgressions. I also had the clear sense that we had run up against the internal wall of how far we could go with this new transparency. There were just certain blockades we could never dismantle.

And, Dad, I also need to tell you one other thing: I'm gay!

No, that was just not going to happen, on that day or ever, with my father. Even if I had been able to admit it to myself—which I had not—he would simply be unable to process that one. Nor could I talk to him about the tremendous damage he had done to me, my brothers, my sisters, and our mom, because I knew he would crack apart under the pressure of such truths. In that moment, I resolved to be thankful for how we'd patched things up. And I simply buried the rest. The real me. All the horrifying dark nights of the past. All of it, for his sake, for my mom and for my siblings, which felt like the right thing to do at the time. I'd finally summoned the courage to stand up to my father in a way I never had.

"I love you, Dad," I said as I leaned in to hug him.

He was crying, but managed to get out, "I love you, too, son." The endearing look he gave me was the first time I ever felt accepted by him. It was the first, only, and last time he said he loved me. Knowing this was a rare connection, I lingered in our hug and relished the feeling as long as I could without making him feel uncomfortable.

From then on, during our visits, my father started opening up about his horrific experiences in World War II, and how he was still haunted by PTSD nightmares of the kamikaze attack on his ship: the commingled burning smell of oil and human beings, the sound of the last dying screams of his shipmates. He talked about the original source of his anger, his own father, which helped me understand where his rage and pain were first set in motion. We started having a workable relationship, which at many points in my life I would have sworn would be impossible. We had actual adult conversations. During one of those conversations Dad promised me one of his most prized possessions, a $10,000 ring he wore daily and had purchased with his entire inheritance when his parents had both died in the sixties. On one trip to Jackpot, Nevada, Dad dropped the ring; he went down on his hands and knees frantically pawing through the dirt. He found it underneath the car behind the front tire. To this day, I still wear the ring on my right-hand ring finger and think of him often.

Despite the light-years we had traversed in improving our relationship, Ben Bolen was still, well, Ben Bolen: full of quirks and oddities no amount of father-son bonding was going to erase. He'd blurt out strange non sequiturs: "You kids are not going to get my money when I die." And while he knew I was wildly successful in business, it was beyond his capacity to give me a simple compliment or "attaboy." Never once did he just say, "Good job, son." He was also the most narcissistic person I have ever met or known, someone who believed his own clotted being was the center around which the entire universe orbited. I expected him to honor my new boundary, which he did. I did not expect him to change. Instead, I focused on what I could control: acceptance of who he was. Forgiveness for what he had done. Back to the basement with Trudy: "It works if you work it. And you're worth it." I'd finally figured out that Dan Bolen was worth it.

WHEN Dad started to fall into the void of dementia, my parents stopped traveling back and forth to Arizona and just stayed in Boise. During one of our talks, I suggested that he should let me help keep an eye on their finances. He was resistant, of course, but also realized he was mentally slipping.

"Dad, just work with me on this," I said. "I want you and Mom to be taken care of for the rest of your lives."

He gave me power of attorney over all their financial affairs, which was a stunning move, and one none of my siblings would have ever believed possible. Dad knew I had a mind for numbers and was trustworthy. He'd let go of the fear that his children were going to steal all his money. Dad had been using a financial advisor, who, as I began poring through everything with my own advisor, turned out to be mostly worthless. He had all Dad's money parked in long-term investments, which didn't make any sense for a man in his eighties. We fired Dad's advisor, reorganized everything, set up automatic monthly bill payments, and watched Mom and Dad's net worth go up. I turned over all their financial assets to my financial advisor, John Pierce, who had been with me for more than twenty years. He did an amazing job for them, and I'm grateful to John to this day for all his guidance.

By 2010, Dad's Alzheimer's disease had all but taken him. There were times he'd be confused.

"This is Danny," I'd say to spark recognition.

"Ah, hi Danny."

His short-term memory was fading, but he was never completely disconnected from who we were. And he could recall other memories, such as his service during World War II. In between my snake-removal and pest-control duties, I would just sit and talk with Dad about his life. He talked a lot about the war. He said when the war ended his commanders ordered that they dump numerous military trucks into the ocean, which angered him as wantonly wasteful.

Sadly, during our visits I could never completely open up to him. Nor could I tell him—or anyone in my family—about my new forbidden love, a beautiful and wonderful woman I had met in Scottsdale.

Part 3
Truth

Sixteen

Are You Free to Remarry?

I HAVE ALWAYS BEEN A FIXER OF OTHER HUMAN beings, first with my family of origin, then in my marriage, with employees, and for friends. At home, at work, and at the congregation, I was the go-to person with all the answers—or at least I thought I was. I rarely gave people time and space to work through their own problems, because I knew what was best. I didn't wait to be asked: I'd see a problem and step in to find a solution.

What I didn't realize is that I was really trying to fix myself by feeding my own ego. *That Dan Bolen is a great guy you can always count on to help.* This orientation caused me to be over-controlling. When I stepped in to fix my daughter's problems, or my wife's, or a fellow JW's, I was getting a bigger boost than they did. And, boy, did I need some boosting after I'd moved to Arizona.

My marriage had failed, which still seemed impossible

because Dan Bolen had never failed at anything… until he did. I was also in full-lockdown denial and still convincing myself I wasn't gay, because that too would be a failure I could not endure. The greatest deceit I've ever committed in this life was hiding from myself, decade after decade. And according to the Jehovah's Witness church doctrine, I was not allowed to remarry again because my divorce was unscriptural, which meant I would have to stay completely celibate, with myself and others, for the rest of my life, without exception. On the one hand, I had gone through so much pain in my marriage and all the years of trying to save it that I initially embraced not ever being able to marry again. Hallelujah! Being barred from getting married wasn't punishment, it was a wonderful blessing that left me thinking, *Who do I thank for this freedom?*

I had seen my parents' marriage, which was unhealthy and toxic, and now I had started, tried to salvage, and ended my own marriage that was even unhealthier. By the late nineties, I did not trust women and would remain happily single for the rest of my days on this earth.

On the other hand, I wasn't thrilled by the strict order of celibacy, including no masturbation, but I somehow accepted the dictate as something I could do to remain a part of my chosen JW family. All my friends were JWs. I spent all my social time with them, doing ministry work and having dinners together. And, believe it or not, after all those years of opposition and hatred, my father had also become a JW and was a pioneer—along with Mom and all six of my siblings, at one time or another. Only because of her, Dad became a JW, and they praised her for sticking it out with him even to the detriment of her own family through the abuse he had administered to all of us. My dad never acknowledged or apologized for any of the abuse, rage, anger, and isolation he gave the family. He wasn't capable of doing that. Narcissists do not apologize, and my dad was a narcissist. Although I couldn't see it at the time, it was like I had fallen into the "Stockholm Syndrome," wherein I grew to know, like, and defend my keeper who told me what I could and could not do, in every facet of my life.

I was crushed that my unscriptural divorce also meant I had to step down as an elder after twenty-five years, which was another blow to my status indicator: I'd failed at marriage and failed my flock. No longer an elder, I was a "publisher" in the congregation. However, I still had a love for Jehovah and the ministry, and believed I was part of something worthwhile. I was taught it was a great honor to be a part of the ministry and share the association of being a publisher. No longer being an elder gave me more time to spend with my brothers and sisters in the organization—but also more time in my addictive work pattern.

In 1998 I bought a two-bedroom patio home in Scottsdale. That same year I hired my brother-in-law Dave Mason, my sister Kay's husband. Dave and Kay were also dedicated JWs who had worked full-time for years in upstate New York in the tiny hamlet of Wallkill, which was part of the world headquarters of Jehovah's Witnesses (the main headquarters was in Brooklyn, New York). Dan Bolen and Associates consisted of the two Ds: I worked out of my office, and my brother-in-law Dave worked out of the spare bedroom. We got along great, because he was just as competitive as I was and had a good personality. I trained him on how to make calls, overcome objections, and close the deals.

"Make the calls and follow the directions I give you," I'd tell him, and he listened. It was difficult work, and he would sweat profusely on calls as I mouthed exactly what he should say. He quickly got more comfortable on his own and became very successful. Within a year Dave and I moved the work operation out of my patio home to a new 2,000-square-foot office space in Scottsdale I'd seen while running along a greenbelt. The interior was completely vacant, so I spent about $100,000 to build it out. We put in four offices, including a large one for me, and a conference room. I had a shower and locker rooms installed, along with a washer and dryer. That way I could do my daily run along the greenbelt (as long as the temperature was below 110 degrees), come back to the office to shower, change, and throw my sweaty clothes in the wash while I went back to work. We bought furniture and artwork, and installed green carpeting. The property landlord was a plastic/oral surgeon who ran his practice next door. Watching his patients come and go from surgeries provided us endless entertainment, as they'd study their puffy and bandaged faces in our mirrored windows without realizing we were watching it all. It was like our own live makeover show, seeing the before-and-after results.

With Dave Mason already on board, I hired a secretary, Janette Clark, who was accurate in her work but painfully slow. We quickly replaced her with Kathy Lennox, a real superstar who never took lunch, had exacting standards, and would crack the whip at all of us, including me. I hired another account executive, Chris Smyth, an attractive woman with perfectly trimmed eyebrows in crescent moons above her eyes. She had been divorced, with two sons, and then remarried. She had a great phone voice and was a woman in a man's world—the heavy industry and male lingo of rotating machinery—who became an amazing recruiter. Chris could hold her own with the boys: you could tell her an inappropriate joke, and she'd laugh and tell you one even more inappropriate.

Jason Scott, who would one day own the place, joined our team in a roundabout way. We had been retained by one of our client companies, and Jason heard about a particular job on his own but was told he had to go through Dan Bolen and Associates. That's when he called me, because he wanted to get out of his job retrofitting vans for disabled people. He interviewed with us and got an offer from the hiring company.

"Before you run my background," he told me, "I just want you to know something's going to come up."

"OK, what is it?"

"I had a DUI in college."

I was impressed by his transparency and getting in front of the issue, just like I trained my people with the FAB sheet: steal any thunder by bringing up any deficiencies first and turning them into an asset. Sure enough, Jason even had a letter from the police department to provide valuable context by documenting that he had been barely over the limit; i.e., legally prohibited from driving but coherent and lucid so that he wasn't endangering anyone.

Now here's a guy we can trust, someone who will tell it to us straight and do the right thing regardless of how it might impact his own situation. The human resources contact at the hiring construction company, however, saw things differently. He took a hardline stance on the single minor blemish and said, "This will be a problem."

I tried everything I could to get Jason hired, but to no avail. Jason was devastated. That's when it hit me.

"You are such an impressive person," I told Jason. "Why don't you come interview to work with us?"

He was elated, and arrived for his interview in a crisp blue suit, white shirt, and tie. We were also interviewing another candidate, Tony Moretto, who had a lot more experience as a vice president of sales in the consumer food industry. Tony was silky smooth, a seemingly born salesman who had the professional look and effortless patter. Ultimately, as much as we all liked Jason, it just made logical sense to hire the experienced sales guy (even though he was overweight, which had triggered my prejudice). Jason was devastated, which he didn't tell me, but he kept the faith and told his wife: "I trust Dan Bolen, and I want to work with him."

Two weeks later, the experienced sales guy turned out to be mostly useless. He said all the right things but avoided making calls; he was more interested in figuring out where to find the best burger at lunch than doing the real work I required. I let him go and called Jason to offer him the job.

My account executives started at a base salary plus commissions, which would put them at roughly $80,000 to

$150,000 in total annual income. On top of that I provided full benefits and put twenty-five percent of their total compensation directly into a profit-sharing account, fully vested in two years. I required my people to give one hundred percent and show up full of passion, so that's why I paid them so well, beyond what any other employer offered.

When I wasn't working, I was at my new congregation in Scottsdale, where various single women showed interest in the new guy from California. But the early whispers cemented my fate: that I'd had an unscriptural divorce and had to step down as an elder after almost twenty-five years. I was the forbidden fruit. I could not date. I could not even call a female JW for a phone conversation; that would violate the rules of my lifelong exile. Because I'm such a people person, this regimented isolation was already taking a heavy toll.

In an attempt to push aside the loneliness and suppress my sexual urges, I embraced my new friends at the Kingdom Hall on Thomas Avenue, where there were about one hundred members. The secretary at my congregation in California had already forwarded my publisher card, which tracked all hours, Bible studies, return visits, and placements (the number of books and brochures distributed) directly to the secretary at the Scottsdale congregation, along with a letter detailing my history including the unscriptural divorce and marriage ban. Despite my scarlet letter, the new members accepted me warmly, including Ray and Ellen Gerhardt. We hit it off, and since I went to three meetings a week, we had a lot of time to chat. Every Tuesday night I attended a book study, and on Thursday night theocratic ministry school and service meetings. Sunday was the public talk and *Watchtower* study. I dived back in, and within four years I was an elder again.

Eventually my new friends Ray and Ellen were bragging about their wonderful daughter who was similarly divorced, had been single for more than twenty years, and lived in Seattle, Washington, where she was director of human resources at a mortgage company. She was also a full-time pioneer/minister. Initially her parents did not know of my unscriptural divorce, and I wasn't volunteering that detail. Still, while their daughter sounded intriguing and I was a powder keg of untapped sexual energy, I knew my unscriptural divorce blackballed any notion of romance. They were selling the amazing features and benefits of luxury air travel to a man on the permanent No-Fly List.

And, of course, no one knew I was gay. I noticed attractive men everywhere I went, and just continued to mentally admonish myself.

I can't do that, so don't think those thoughts.
Don't look.
Don't go there.

It was a wrenching turmoil that never subsided. I could temporarily tamp down the urges by burying myself at work, by being a great speaker at the congregation, and being the perfect Dan. All great distractions. Constant motion and never a spare moment to stop and reflect. But my energies were all jumbled. I'd give a moving spiritual talk to the flock and then, while out at dinner together afterward, I'd be noticing the good-looking guy at the next table.

I can't do that, so don't think those thoughts.
Don't look.
Don't go there.

When you're not allowed to be yourself, you thrive on sneaking glances at attractive men. Concurrently, in 2004—as I passed the seven-year itch mark after my divorce—the big moment arrived at a JW circuit assembly held at a school.

"Dan," my friend Ray said, "this is our daughter Sandy from Seattle. Sandy, this is Dan."

There had been a long and steady build-up to this moment, so the chances of being let down were extremely high. However, when we exchanged smiles, I knew immediately I was in trouble. If anything, she dazzled more than her parents had let on. Of course, she was dressed modestly, and she was very slender with tousled brown hair that fell just below her ears. She had a radiant smile with beautiful teeth.

"Hi, Sandy. I've heard a lot of good things about you."

"Likewise."

From that moment we hit it off famously. When the assembly ended later that day, her parents invited me to their house to join them for dinner. Since her parents were going to be there, and we would not be alone together per the church rules, I gladly accepted. I thanked them for the invite and went home to change.

It was July in Phoenix, so I showed up at their house in shorts, a T-shirt, and flip-flops. When her father greeted me wearing slacks, a dress shirt, and a smoking jacket with a silk ascot around his neck, I was mortified. The dog Molly even had an ascot! The table was set elegantly for a formal dinner, with all the flatware and utensils arranged to perfection. Classical music filled the house; he was an accomplished musician and music instructor who had given Steven Spielberg trumpet lessons in Phoenix where Spielberg grew up and shot his early movies. Somehow, my wardrobe gaffe did nothing to diminish our easy conversation through dinner.

"Oh, Dan," Sandy's mom said. "I'm so sorry I overcooked the ham."

"No, it's perfect." I figured out later that's how she got her compliments. To her, food was love. The food was delicious, and I grew to truly love Ellen.

After dinner, Sandy and I went to the kitchen alone to do the dishes. We each opened up about our respective divorces. She had been married twelve years. Her husband had had an affair and mired them in debt. She was in her early forties, was industrious, dedicated to her work, and loved people. She enjoyed exercise, including spinning class and running, and had worked hard to reorient her financial ship after the divorce. She had done so by working full-time as a minister, moving in with her brother and his family to save money; after seven years she had paid off all the debts from her marriage. To that end, she had been especially selective in her dating life; no way she was going to wander back into another unhealthy union.

For her part, she confessed her parents loved me, and her mother especially had been extolling the virtues of Dan Bolen to Sandy for months and months. Sandy loved my "radio announcer" voice and that I wore jewelry. That first "date" (which we could not officially call a date, because I was prohibited from such craven acts) with her parents as chaperones, like we were 13 again, could not have gone any better. Several days later Sandy called and asked the million-dollar question, "Dan, are you free to remarry?"

"No, Sandy, unfortunately I am not."

That she'd gone from meeting me for the first time to a few days later mentioning marriage didn't faze me at all. I was equally intrigued by this woman. Without the church's blessing, however, I was tainted goods. The proverbial forbidden fruit. What she said next really hit home.

"Because if you are," she said, "I'd like to pursue a relationship."

Light bulb: I started to consider what had once been unthinkable. *I may actually consider remarrying.* Since Sandy had her scriptural freedom and I did not, we would have to tightrope the logistics and rules of our interactions, because I could not "date" her. We instead became friends and, in every way, confidantes. I was attracted to her physical beauty, which was a no-brainer because she was in great shape, with classic features, but also her emotional and spiritual beauty—including the way she took care of her parents. She lived in Seattle, so when calling her on the telephone, the conversations were all categorized under the guise of official JW business. When she did visit Phoenix to see her parents about every six weeks, we could not be alone together in the same car. We could not kiss, touch each other in any way, or hold hands. I could not even go home, fantasize about this beautiful woman, and masturbate. All forbidden because of my grave sin, the unscriptural divorce. And, yet, I honored that extreme rigidity and the inhumane rules because I did not want to lose my JW family, the one Bruce Benson had brought me into almost forty years prior at college.

Even so, small cracks were starting to appear in my bedrock blind faith. I started to have issues with certain stories, such as Sodom and Gomorrah. It really bothered me that the Jehovah's Witnesses did not condemn Lot for offering his daughters to the raging mob; apparently that was OK? What decent father would give up his daughters to have sex with a mob? And our Jehovah was going to destroy everyone deemed unrighteous during Armageddon? That one didn't make any sense to me either, because as JWs we protested war and professed peace and non-violence. Yet our God was ready to slaughter everyone who wasn't JW? These questions started to trouble me, but I never spoke a word of it. Instead, I pushed the thoughts away and tried to focus on the good I saw in what we were doing.

OVER the next few years, as my dad's condition worsened and I started making trips to Boise to eradicate bugs and snakes, I decided I was all in with Sandy and would try to get my scriptural freedom from my ex-wife. This would be the JW version of taking my case to the court of appeals. I asked the elders to follow up and reconsider; they said they would, but they did not. I started to see a harsh truth within "the truth" they professed: If the issue at hand did not concern them, their families, or their closest friends, they exhibited almost no urgency, care, or effort. I ended up fighting my spiritual appeals battle for nine years. I never did get my freedom.

The woman I truly loved with all my heart and wanted to marry could only be—officially—my good friend. And, more painfully, she could never be anything more.

Unless I left the Jehovah's Witnesses.

Seventeen

The Death Rattle

IN 2006, LIKE THE GOOD CHRISTIAN SOLDIER I professed to be, I was still toeing the hard line in my attempts to please Jehovah and my chosen family at the congregation. To do so, however, meant adhering to more rules that made no sense and, sadly, were demeaning to the woman I had grown to love.

When Sandy and I went with a group to Mexico to preach the good news, we were not allowed to be a couple because of my unscriptural divorce. That meant we could not ever be alone together or touch each other in any way, including holding hands. We were two consenting adults in a committed, loving relationship (officially just a friendship) who had never physically touched each other. Not a light touch on her arm, or a hug, and certainly not a kiss. Nothing. We couldn't even be seen together, just the two of us, at breakfast in the hotel lobby. But the absurdity did not end there. Since we were both fitness enthusiasts, when we had some down time on our trip we took the opportunity to go for a run together on the public beach in San Carlos.

"We can't run together," I reluctantly said as we laced up our running shoes.

"I know," she said, smiling. "It's OK."

So instead, she let me take the lead as I trotted out across the sand. Once I had a head start, she dropped in about twenty yards behind me. We did our entire run that way, with her trailing behind me so that we weren't a couple. The entire display embarrassed and bothered me. And yet I was still shackled to doing what others told me I had to do, which was how I kept my church family intact.

Glory be to Jehovah in the highest: look at our unfailing dedication and willingness to demean one of your children, a strong, independent woman, all in your name!

One of my sisters, who was on the trip, saw us running and scolded me later for the obvious affection Sandy and I had for each other, despite our best attempts to conceal our mutual admiration. By then I'd been a part of the Jehovah's Witnesses organization for forty years. When you're in a group that long and fully bonded to the members—and the tremendous affirmation and sense of belonging that membership brings—you don't realize that you've actually traded away parts of yourself just to stay in the group. Who you really are distorts to match the image held up by the group's norms and rules. I had no perspective or context to realize any of this at the time, but being part of the Jehovah's Witnesses had risen to the same toxic level of blind loyalty.

Blood in, blood out.

Like Jim Jones's followers had demonstrated, I was willing to drink the Kool-Aid for the cause. I was not ready to consider the C-word to describe what was happening—the worst word one might ascribe to an organized group. But indeed, like so many others who find themselves trapped in contradictory and limiting ideologies, I was a member of a cult without even realizing it. I'd been reshaped by the slow drip, drip, drip of the messaging (brainwashing) over decades. Adhering to the group's rules, including the non-contact policy, was not getting any easier as I saw Sandy in a one-piece pink swimsuit on that same trip. She looked amazing, I had strong feelings for her—emotionally, physically, and spiritually—and I could not express these emotions since we were barred from being anything other than good friends.

Then, while on that trip Sandy and I got some terrible news: her father, Ray Gerhardt, who was also my dear friend, had terminal cancer.

THE end was upon us quickly, as Ray's multiple myeloma spread and his condition deteriorated rapidly. Ray was a kind and loving man, more stoic than emotionally expressive. He was proper and well-organized. He was a true music lover and concert violinist who had performed with Nancy Wilson, Eddie Arnold, Sammy Davis Jr., and Barbra Streisand in A *Star is Born*. Sandy started making more frequent trips from Seattle to Scottsdale to be with her dad; consequently, we were seeing a lot of each other, too. Each time I had an overwhelming urge to comfort her with a simple hug. But according to the dictates of my chosen religion, even a hug offered in kindness was taboo.

Home hospice care was the final stage. The night Ray died I was at Sandy's parents' house with a small group that included her mom, Sandy, one of her sisters, and several JW friends. It was a peaceful, reverential moment as Ray passed, one that Sandy and I had had time to brace for, which helped but did not diminish the impact and sadness. In the moment, without censoring myself, I held Sandy's hand as her father took his last breath. Then I gave her a hug as she cried and grieved. Offering this physical contact at the time of Sandy's greatest loss was the humane thing to do. One of the church sisters paid careful attention to our touching, and later she spread the gossip of our human connectedness. Soon everyone in the congregation knew, and the news bubbled up the command chain to the elders: Dan Bolen and Sandy Gerhardt were interested in each other. *Very interested.* Thereafter we were under constant and heavy scrutiny.

In holding Sandy's hand, I was trying to show compassion to someone who had just lost her father, which I would have done for any fellow congregation member, male or female. Thereafter, the elders would scrutinize us for our grave transgression, because I was forbidden from such touching due to my unscriptural divorce.

Blood in, blood out.

Both Ray and Ellen loved me, but because they were also Jehovah's Witnesses, they had supported the official stand of the church that prohibited me from marrying their daughter, which they would have otherwise eagerly blessed. Likewise, nosy women from the congregation and the by-the-book male elders were unceasingly scrutinizing us. The only way Sandy and I could connect without being watched was through covert telephone calls. And by then I didn't care that our phone calls broke church rules: Sandy and I connected through our many long phone calls. With her father gone, I made sure to look out for her mother, and I let Sandy know how she was faring with those regular phone calls.

I saw her mom, Ellen, at the congregation, and Sandy knew every Monday night I went to her mom's house to watch *Dancing with the Stars* with her. She'd always have a snack ready, and we'd watch the show together, catch up on church gossip, and laugh as she reminisced about Sandy as a little girl growing up in Paradise Valley, Arizona. I guess because Ellen was older, and was like a mother to me, I assumed it was all right that we were alone together in her house without supervision. In fact, we were probably violating more church rules. I even used to give Ellen foot rubs while we watched television, because it helped her relax. I had a deep love for her as one of my older sisters in the congregation. She, too, had found a new family in JW as I had.

On my calls to update Sandy, we would often still be talking two hours later. Did I feel guilty that I was "phone dating" and once again breaking the rules? No, because I had decided some of these rules were just silly. Two consenting adults, who live in two different states and care deeply about each other, can't have a phone conversation? Forget that.

Regardless, other than our secret phone calls, we felt the constant pressure of being watched by the congregation members, like two offenders on the run just waiting to be officially indicted for our crimes. Indeed, when a new providing overseer named Scott Matthews came into the congregation, an obese man who had the backing and blessing of the circuit overseer, it was only a matter of time. Scott had heard the rumors about Sandy and me and our wicked ways *(they held hands and hugged in her house while her dad died!)*, so he was determined to take me out. Then, after I'd caught him in a lie and exposed the truth to the circuit overseer, Scott made it his personal mission to take down Dan Bolen.

Sure enough, Scott came at me and got the support of the other elders, and they asked me to step down as an elder for the second time in my life. It was a hurtful indignation after years of clawing my way back to elder status at the new congregation in Scottsdale. The circuit overseer, however, had my back and asked if I wanted to appeal the decision, which would have required me going before the council of elders (including Scott). Instead, I was exhausted from being under the heat of investigation for so many years. Maybe, I thought, if I resigned as an elder they would just leave Sandy and me alone. And, quite frankly, I was so frustrated and depressed, I just did what they asked and gave up my elder role because I didn't have the emotional energy to fight it. At church, the speaker made a vague announcement, "Dan Bolen is no longer an elder," and then moved on without any other explanation, as though he'd just mentioned the date of a bake sale. How quickly and easily they had cast me aside, someone who had dedicated most of his adult life to the Jehovah's

Witnesses. I felt embarrassed that I had failed again as an elder. And Dan Bolen didn't like to fail at anything. And yet I stayed in the organization because I was hard-wired to follow their rules.

Blood in, blood out.

IF things came in threes, Sandy and I were about to face our second big loss in July 2011. By then my father was 87. His dementia had worsened, he'd suffered several strokes, and he was only getting more ill. That month my older brother and sisters and their husbands traveled from Boise to a JW convention in Washington state. Knowing they would be gone, I traveled from Arizona to Boise to see my mom and help look after my dad. By then Dad was in the locked memory care unit at the facility. When none of us children could be with him, Mom would spend the entire day there so he wasn't alone. But he always got agitated when she had to leave at night. During my visit that July, one of the unit nurses greeted me at the door.

"He's not doing well," she said, and I knew what she meant. Dad hadn't been doing well for years, but no one had ever just said it straight out. I braced myself and went to his room, where Mom was sitting with another sister from the congregation. I smiled at both and hugged my mom. Then I went to my dad.

"Hi Dad, it's Danny," I said, taking his hand. "I just want to tell you how much I love you."

He turned and looked at me and managed a faint smile, but I'm not sure he recognized me. His lips were dry and cracked. His skin looked transparent. He squeezed my hand. From that moment, and through the next twenty-four hours, I sent regular text messages to my sisters and my older brother to keep them updated. I pulled up a chair and sat by his bed and studied the face of the man I had hated with such dark intensity.

Now all I saw was a frail man, stripped bare to his basic humanity, vulnerable. I smiled as I recalled the big summit I'd convened over hamburgers at TGI Friday's, and then got teary-eyed when I thought about him crying for the first time, right there at our table still cluttered with our lunch plates. We had traversed light-years in our relationship over the last eleven years of his life. And no, what we had was never going to be The Waltons.

Good night, Dad.

Good night, Danny!

He could *never* know I was gay; if he had, he never would have accepted it. At that moment, I had not even accepted it. My father almost certainly would have entirely rejected me just as I was still rejecting myself, cut off from the real me behind a towering wall of work and church success.

Instead, we had forged an imperfect way forward that worked. We did the best we could with what we had, and by the end we were father and son, connected and in a loving place. Then I recalled a time after that summit, after Dad had granted me power of attorney and had entrusted me to manage his financial affairs.

"Danny," he'd proudly said one day, "I want to invest in pay telephone booths. It's going to be huge. I met a guy who told me all about it."

I laughed aloud. "Good one, Dad." Except I could see by the look on his face that he was serious. "Dad, cell phones. It's a new millennium." I held mine up just to be sure he knew the devices existed, minus any wires, and that pay telephones were disappearing faster than cotton candy at a state fair.

"Danny, will you just talk to the guy?"

"Yes, Dad, I'll talk to him, and then I'll tell him you're not giving him a penny of your money, and then I'll tell him a second time: no!"

A few days later I did, in fact, meet with the guy, who drove up in an old Rolls-Royce with a wheel that squeaked. When he climbed out of the car in a wrinkled three-piece suit, he had a hundred-dollar-bill dangling strategically from his front jacket pocket. *Good Lord*, I thought. *Is this guy serious with the cheesy prop car and prop cash?*

"Don't you say a word," I'd told the supposed investor. "I'm instructing my father not to give you a single dollar, let alone the $10,000 you want."

So, yes, of course Dad had eagerly handed over the ten grand to the cheesy investor, promptly lost it all, and never mentioned it to me again.

DAD'S death rattle startled me out of my reverie. A nurse came in and dabbed morphine on his lips with a cotton ball.

"He could pass any time now," she said.

It was late afternoon, with the long rays of summer sunshine beaming through the gaps in the closed blinds and illuminating the dust motes suspended in the air. We sat watching Dad breathe, and then he stopped breathing. Crying, I hugged him, told him again how much I loved him, and said goodbye. Then I called each of my siblings except Dean, who had died earlier that year in Mexico.

Ben Bolen, born in 1923 in Cape Fair, Missouri, World War II veteran, died July 8, 2011. And, yes, despite the amazing distances we had covered in improving our relationship, Ben Bolen had always been, well, Ben Bolen—full of quirks, oddities, and strange investment strategies no amount of father-son bonding was going to erase.

Eighteen

It's Who I Am

ALTHOUGH SANDY'S MOM HAD HEART HEALTH issues, Ellen Gerhardt lived another five years after her beloved Ray died. Sandy lived in Seattle, but she came to Scottsdale every four to six weeks and stayed with her mom to take her to doctor appointments and help around the house. Because of those visits to see her mom, Sandy and I saw each other regularly despite living 1,400 miles apart. When Sandy returned to Seattle, usually after about a week in Arizona, I took the baton to look after Ellen, including our weekly *Dancing with the Stars* visits. The year 2012, however, would shatter both the regularity of that interstate routine and some of my own long-standing inertia. In other words, things were about to get real… real fast.

That is, I was finally taking the first step in sharing the secret I had been guarding for fifty-eight years, the one I had pledged I would take to my grave. Before that milestone, though: While Sandy was on one of her regular trips to Scottsdale to visit her mom, she went out for her daily run. When she came back her mom said her chest was hurting. Sandy dialed 9-1-1 and ran into the other room to grab her purse. She was still in her running gear when the sound of sirens was audible.

"Oh my God, Sandy," her mother said.

"What is it, Mom?"

"Are you going to wear that to the hospital?"

Sandy could only smile and shake her head. The paramedics arrived and rushed Ellen to the hospital but, unfortunately Ellen quickly passed from this life. Because of what had happened when her dad died—when I had violated church rules by holding Sandy's hand and hugging her—she didn't call me until after her mom had died. Not having a chance to say goodbye to Ellen crushed my heart and soul.

"Why didn't someone call me?" I said through my tears while on the phone with Sandy.

She paused and then said, "I'm sorry. You understand."

"Right," I said, crying, but figuring it out. "It would have been an issue."

My brother-in-law Dave Mason, who still worked for me and was married to my sister Kay, was the minister at Ellen's funeral just as he had been for Ray. Between Sandy and me, our only surviving parent was my mother, who lived in Boise.

After her mom's passing, Sandy came to Scottsdale for an extended time to wrap up her mom's final affairs. Despite our rigid adherence to the rules—no touching, no hugging, no dating, no illicit phone contact—people were noticing our undeniable bond. I regularly got strong counsel and was reminded of the importance of being a good example to the flock. For Sandy and me, the pressure of denying our true feelings had been building for years. We had fallen in love but couldn't express it publicly, and we certainly couldn't do anything privately, either, because if we acted on our impulses we would have both been cast out, disfellowshipped from the congregation. While we did our best in public to ignore each other, in 2012 I had reached my breaking point. Sandy and I had been doing this dance for eight years, in love and unable to openly embrace that love.

"I'm in love with you," I told her on the phone one night.

"I feel the same way."

"We need to break it off, Sandy," I said, crying. "I just can't take it anymore, because seeing you while having to stay cut off from you is just too painful."

"I know," she said through her own tears. "We also both know we have to follow the rules of the church."

While we were both rule-followers, I was a little more willing to bend the rules than she was. But she was right: We couldn't be together because of my unscriptural divorce, which I had unsuccessfully tried numerous times to reverse by providing information to the church that the elders never followed up on. She and I would forever be forbidden fruit to each other if we both wanted to continue as Jehovah's Witnesses. And I had to continue, because this was my family.

"Goodbye, Sandy," I said, crying. "I love you."

"I love you, too, Dan. I will always love you."

We hung up, and it felt like I was tumbling backward into a dark void. This was not a teenage crush, an unrequited longing, but since I was late to the game I would still experience all the desperate sadness at 65 years old. Despite some of my increasing doubts and questions about the Jehovah's Witness rigidity, I was still willing to sacrifice the woman I loved to remain in the family that was my emotional anchor.

Blood in, blood out.

THUS began a mostly miserable year in my life, marked by an expansive emptiness and loneliness. Although we had never seen each other daily or even weekly, Sandy had been a regular part of my life for eight years. Now we had broken up a relationship that never officially existed, and with both her parents gone and all their affairs wrapped up, Sandy had no reason to travel to Arizona. I was never going to see her at the congregation or otherwise run into her at the store, gym, or anywhere else. I had lost Ray, Ellen and my dad, and now Sandy was gone, too. I had lost the love of her entire family.

The psychic pain of such a loss was tremendous. I attempted to deal with the pain as I always had, by pouring my energies into exercising more than two hours daily and taking on more at church, including giving public talks at several congregations (on behalf of the faith that had robbed me of my college education and now Sandy). And, of course, I tried to fill every other spare moment with my secular work.

Even by 2012, working more was still giving me the same adrenaline rush and all-consuming hit. I wasn't traveling anymore or running around the country giving recruiting seminars. But the Dan Bolen and Associates team I had assembled was humming along like a precision machine.

During this time, there was never a dull moment with our candidates. We had a top-notch vice president of operations who had moved to a company in Washington state that would lead him up the org chart to president. He had accepted the job, at an outstanding salary, and had been working there for two weeks while waiting for his wife and children to join him from Texas. One day I got a call from the woman. She was hysterically screaming.

"My husband has to quit!" she said, crying.

"Who are you, and what are you talking about?"

She frantically gave me her name and said, "You pulled my husband away from our family and friends in Texas. Please make him quit."

There was an odd echo during this phone call. "Where are you?" I asked.

"My cell phone died, so I'm in a phone booth." Perhaps it was one my dad had invested in, because the audio quality was terrible.

"I'm sure we can work this out," I said.

"No, you need to get him to quit, because the dog just vomited all over me and the car and the kids, and I can't take this anymore!"

"I can assure you this is a normal part of the process, because this is a big life stressor you're experiencing. It's going to be fine. I know you're upset. I know you're concerned. Let me call your husband, and we're going to sort this out."

When I called the husband, he told me that she had regular mental breakdowns, and he knew exactly how to calm her down. He did; she moved with the children, and the entire family fell in love with Washington.

Another time, my recruiter Chris Smyth had an excellent candidate for a district manager job with a major pump company in Texas. After the initial phone interview, the hiring company loved the candidate and wanted to fly him to Houston for a personal interview. When the candidate called Chris, he said he had something to tell her.

"I need to be open and honest with you and my prospective employer."

"OK," Chris said. "That's great."

"I'm in the process of being transgendered from a man to a woman."

Chris didn't know what to say. She was as shocked as his own family and children had been when he told them. But his family was supportive, and so was Chris. In this sales position, the candidate would be calling on clients as a man initially, and then over time as he transitioned, he would begin arriving as a woman.

"I want to tell the employer during my interview."

"Well, hold on, let me talk to my manager and get back to you."

Chris came running into my office and explained the situation. "So do we tell the employer, or have him tell them?"

I thought about it: both we and the hiring company needed to be careful about discrimination. "He needs to tell them."

He traveled to Texas and went to the interview. When Chris called the hiring company after the interview, they said the candidate was very capable, although he seemed a bit nervous. However, they wanted to make him an offer for the job.

"Did he tell you anything else?" Chris asked.

"Not really."

"Nothing?" Chris wondered if she had a duty to report what they'd discussed.

"Oh," the hiring manager said. "You mean that he's being transgendered?"

"Yes."

"That's not a problem for us, because the boss he'll be working for is already transgendered, and we have another transgender person on staff as well."

Through it all, I had started – *gasp!* – taking some Fridays off to just sit and reflect on my life and what might be next. With Sandy out of the picture and time on my hands, as I started to get somewhat sober from my work addiction, an age-old question bubbled to the surface.

Who is Dan Bolen?

As always, I viewed this existential uncertainty as a problem, which was good—because as a problem-solver I could switch my focus back to fixing. And who better to fix an emotional glitch than a good therapist? For several years I had known Ron Mitchell, who lived in my subdivision that was built around a manufactured lake. Ever since I'd met Ron, I had been quietly taking mental notes. First, he was openly gay and lived with his husband without apology or shame. This was a real eye-opener to me, and showed that it was possible, at least for other people not named Dan Bolen. Ron and his husband would lazily float by my backyard on their little pontoon boat and wave "hello" while raising their cocktail glasses. I'd smile and wave back.

Yes, that's what a gay couple looks like!

Ron was a super-nice, fit, and an attractive blond guy who also synchronously (for my purposes) happened to be a therapist. If ever there was a human being on planet Earth with whom I would feel safe prying open locked doors within myself, it was Ron Mitchell. Even so, I still wasn't even sure I would be able to voice what I had long professed I would never utter aloud: that I was attracted to men. Yes, even at 65 I could not yet admit to myself that I was gay, only that I was attracted to men.

My workaround was to call Ron and make my first session appointment under the guise of wanting to discuss my work addiction, which was partially true but mostly a way to dip my toe in the waters of what might, or might not, be safe to share. Would I be able to tell Ron I was attracted to men? I put the chances at seventy/thirty against. But let's be clear: No way I was ever telling anyone I was gay, because I wasn't!

Our first session went well. I did, indeed, have a work addiction that I no longer wanted to control my life. I told him about my sadness about breaking up with the woman I loved, and how painful it was to not see or speak to Sandy. I talked about the stress at work that came with running one's own company, and that I wanted to start planning my exit from that company and my eventual retirement. As I sat there talking to Ron, I wanted to tell him about my "attraction to men" (although I was not gay!), because I knew he'd understand. I wanted to tell him the story about the attractive young guy I had noticed at L.A. Fitness who was in my step class and noticed me, too. I wanted to tell him that later, when I walked up to my white 1999 Porsche Boxster (which I still have to this day) there was a note from the young guy under the wiper blade: *I'd love to go have a drink with you sometime. Give me a call.*

I wanted to tell Ron that I took out my cell phone right there on the spot, dialed the number the cute guy had written, and left a voicemail: "Thank you for your note. But I need to let you know I'm a heterosexual man." See, I could be attracted and not gay! And, yes, interesting that I had to call the young man to put it on the record that I was not ready to make a buy decision, only endlessly browsing.

I wondered, too, as I sat in Ron's office, whether he saw through all of it and could look into my heart with his well-trained therapist gaze, not to mention his highly tuned "gaydar," and see the true Dan Bolen. I had that passing thought repeatedly as we met several times, while I continued to dance around the real reason I was there at $122 per hour. Then, finally, during my fourth session, I broached the subject.

"Ron, there's something I need to tell you."

"Dan, you know this is a safe space and anything you say is confidential."

"Mmm," was all I could mutter.

Ron smiled. "What did you want to tell me?"

Nothing, I thought. *Still time to bolt for the door and never return.*

"Dan?"

I hesitated, and wondered if I could do this after a lifetime of deep denial. I had pushed my own truth so far down that I didn't know whether it was even still accessible. There was still time to turn and run, to push the rising turmoil back down again and live out my life as I had been doing. I was 65: I had mastered the delicate walk of looking but not touching and living a successful life. Why pull the pin on a hand grenade and throw it into my well-ordered world now, at my advancing age? This was the new century, when people confronted their identity issues in their teens and twenties, not their sixties. And what, exactly, was my identity?

At my innermost core was the secret I had kept from Dad so he didn't kill me, literally or figuratively. The secret I had guarded at the congregation for decades and through my first marriage. The secret I'd kept hidden from my daughter, my loving first Al Anon group in the basement, and my life-saving men's support group at Betty Ford. The secret I'd hidden throughout my entire professional career, from everyone I'd ever worked with and for, on the phone, in person, and at conferences and seminars. Who would I be without the secret? Because I had become the secret.

Then an immense sadness almost swallowed me whole, right

there, because I realized I had spent my entire life pretending to be someone other than who I really was, which meant I had lived a duplicitous life; despite all I professed to be at home, work, and church, I was nothing more than a bargain-rate con man, a phony, a fake, and a liar.

"Where'd you just go, Dan?"

"What?"

"What's coming up for you?" Ron asked.

"Just… everything," I said. And when I said "everything," I meant it, as my entire life spooled past my eyes in a fast-forward loop, a sadly inauthentic life. I was the door-to-door World Book encyclopedia salesman who had perfected the patter of presenting a conjured version of Dan Bolen that made everyone happy, but left me alone and empty.

"My heart's racing," I said. "My mind's spinning."

"You're safe now, Dan. You're safe here with me."

Although I'm not sure how or why, those words uncorked something in me that I'd been lugging around my entire life. The floodgates opened: I cried and then sobbed like I've never let loose. My father had terrified me, and I'd been running from that terror since I was a child, always in motion, always working, exercising, preaching, striving, fixing, people-pleasing, and then for good measure doubling down… more achieving, and then working, exercising, preaching, striving, fixing, people-pleasing, a never-ending Hell on Earth I'd been running until that exact moment in time and space when Ron threw me the safety rope and pulled me out of the fire. Where I could finally just sit down and let go and breathe for the first time without taking another step. Then I just said the words: "I *may be* attracted to men."

Ron played a perfect poker face and nodded. "You *may* be?"

I nodded.

"Is that OK?" he asked.

"I'm not sure."

"Do you know I'm gay?" Ron asked

"Yes."

"Now that you know me as being gay, do you still like me?"

"Of course."

Ron got up and went to his whiteboard. Like a good football coach diagramming a play, he sketched the x's and o's: *Dan is a good man. Dan is attracted to men.*

"Are those two statements true?" he asked.

"Yes."

"OK, then how about this?" He wrote: *Dan is bad because he's attracted to men.*

"That's where I struggle," I said.

"I would say if you believe that, it's your shame talking, not reality."

I nodded. That made sense. Except... easier said than done.

"What would have to happen for it to be OK for you to be attracted to men?"

"That's a good question," I said.

"How long have you felt this attraction?" he asked.

"Since I was 7."

"Does that give you any insight?"

I tried unsuccessfully to hold back more tears. "It's who I am."

"And who are you?"

I looked at him and nodded. "I think I'm bisexual." I had the sensation of being 1,000 feet above that room, floating at the edge of outer space and watching this scene unfold: did that 65-year-old man just say I think I'm bisexual, to another human being? *Wait, is that Dan Bolen down there saying such things aloud? And, more importantly, to himself?*

Then I was freefalling and back in the room with Ron, when he said, "Why do you think you're bisexual, Dan?"

"I've been married and have a child. I also truly love Sandy, and would like to marry her if I could. But I'm also attracted to men. Am I bisexual?" In telling Ron I was bisexual, my biggest fear was that I was cutting off any possibility of ever being with

Sandy, because I knew that would never work for her.

"Dan, our sexuality is almost never one hundred percent gay or straight. Everything is on a spectrum. Some people might be ninety percent straight and ten percent gay. Or maybe seventy percent gay and thirty percent straight. Others are predominantly gay and would never act on their heterosexual attractions. Have you ever considered that you're somewhere on that spectrum?"

Then I blurted out words I never thought I'd say: "Given a choice, I'd probably choose a man over a woman."

Well, there you go, Dan Bolen. Now you've done it; you just put it out there into the world where you can't pull it back. Ever. You just said it aloud to another human being! Are you sure you want to do this? Really, now, just what in the hell are you doing here?

Ron just smiled. Unlike my own, his energy was comforting, soothing, and accepting, which made me realize I felt safe with everything I had just unloaded after carrying it around for a lifetime. I also had a strong conviction—*He thinks I'm gay!*—and I'm glad he didn't voice a direct question to make me testify on the record. I still couldn't quite go there, at least not on that day. Or maybe ever. But it did make me wonder...

Was I gay?

Nineteen

Half-Relieved and Half-Terrified

WHEN SANDY'S NEPHEW'S 5-YEAR-OLD SON JAKE tragically lost his battle with liver cancer, the funeral would be held in Scottsdale. I heard the news and, after not having any contact for almost a year, sent Sandy a text message to express my condolences. We exchanged text messages, and she told me she was coming to Arizona for the funeral. I told her I wanted to be there to support her and her family. She was receptive to my offer. Our digital conversation stirred up a jumble of emotions in me: sadness for her loss, longing for her presence, and an unmistakable deep love for her that had not faded despite not having any contact for so long.

The funeral was on a Saturday, with a large turnout. When I saw Sandy, my heart leapt. She looked great, as always.

"I'm so sorry you lost Jake," I told her. It was a beautiful service and a somber day of reflection. The next morning I called Sandy at her hotel.

"I'd like to see you before you go back," I told her, "but today I need to go to Payson."

Sandy's response floored me.

"I'd like to go to Payson with you," she said.

She had to be joking, right? Some years earlier I had bought a second home in Payson, which was an hour and a half northeast of my Scottsdale home in a cooler mountain climate. I was now part of the Payson congregation, after leaving the original one I had joined in Scottsdale. I would drive up to Payson for meetings on Thursday night, Saturday ministry, and Sunday public talk and *Watchtower* study, and then return to Scottsdale late Sunday or early Monday.

"You know you're not allowed to do that," I said.

"I'd like to go with you."

I was shocked. The two of us alone in a car for hours on an out-of-town excursion would be an overt snub to the church and all their rules against us "dating." But she didn't have to ask again, because I was thrilled.

I picked her up for the drive, and we behaved perfectly throughout: We didn't hug, touch, or hold hands, and certainly didn't kiss. We had an amazing conversation that flowed so easily it just seemed we were meant to be together. Although it was Sunday, with the memorial service I had taken the weekend off from my normal church duties. After I took care of a few things at my house in Payson, we drove back late Sunday afternoon as dusk fell. As we neared Scottsdale and the twinkling cityscape, I floated another forbidden idea.

"Would you like to come to my house?" I asked. "We'll just sit out on the patio and have a cocktail."

"Okay," she said. "As long as we just sit outside."

Like two teenagers whose parents had forbidden us to see each other, we knew what all the coded talk meant. We weren't just tiptoeing around the church rules now with phone calls under the guise of official church business. We were violating the spirit and the letter of the laws, and while we both felt twinges of guilt, we were going to do it anyway. The perfect storm was gathering. We sat on my back patio by the lake, water feature trickling and music playing. I half wondered if my gay friend Ron Mitchell might float by on his boat with his husband and raise a glass.

See, Ron, I could shout, *I am bisexual, attracted to men and women!*

We each had a martini, continued to push away our respective guilt about breaking the church rules, and thoroughly enjoyed our conversation. But it was all just too much to bear, and something finally snapped inside me.

"I can't do this anymore," I said, standing up. "I love you, but I can't have you. I want to marry you, Sandy, so you're going to have to make your choice."

That was the moment the dam broke. Our year apart had been extremely difficult. We had tried to follow the rules and make everyone happy, including the congregation members and the elders… everyone but ourselves. We always had to put on the pretense of doing the right thing, by the book, and relegate our own needs to last place. I just couldn't do it anymore.

I had separated from my first wife in 1994, with the divorce final in 1996. That meant I'd lived eighteen years of rigid dogma and sexual anorexia, including nine years of repressed urges and deprivation with Sandy. I'd only masturbated three times during all that time: I had more willpower than the Asgardian Thunder God Thor. Likewise, throughout that time I'd never acted on my attraction to men (not since that time when I was 13). What I'd endured was record-breaking levels of deprivation that was inhumane: I had lost my sexuality completely. Half-relieved and half-terrified at what I'd just voiced to the woman I loved, I walked into the house.

Sandy followed, moved toward me, and said: "Let's just get married."

We embraced, which was only the second time we'd ever physically touched. The first time was when her father passed away and I'd held her hand.

Now, nothing else needed to be said. For the first time ever, after knowing, cherishing, and loving each other for nine years, we kissed. Talk about a long build-up to the world's most anticipated kiss… which was beyond heavenly. With that, I had my answer.

Sandy and I were going to get married.

By the next morning, Monday, November 7, things were already moving quickly. Sandy was staying at a hotel in Scottsdale and extended her stay. She had to call her brother, who owned the mortgage company where she worked part-time, to tell him she needed to stay longer, but she didn't say why. Since we had told no one of our plans, we were the only two who knew she had come to Arizona for a funeral and was staying to get married. While Sandy made her call, I called Ron Mitchell, who said he was available if we could keep our call under fifteen minutes. I told him what I had come up with on my own.

"Ron, I'm sixty percent gay and forty percent heterosexual. I love this woman and want to marry her, but she doesn't know that I'm sixty percent gay."

"How does that make you feel?"

"Well, I'm wondering if I need to tell her."

"You can tell her, Dan. Or you can also live a great life, with her, in the forty percent."

Up to that point, my greatest regret in life was dropping out of college to join my new family of Jehovah's Witnesses. But in the next moment, I was about to make a decision that would later move to the top of my list of greatest regrets. And all I needed to tip the scales was Ron Mitchell's blessing. While Ron's counsel might seem out of step today, I don't dismiss his views as incorrect, because he was just suggesting that life is not black and white, gay or straight, yes or no. He was giving me options, to be genuine and make my own choices. And because of that freedom I was about to enjoy some wonderful years with a woman I truly loved.

In hindsight, however, I was not being fully transparent and truthful with Sandy, the woman I loved deeply. The pain of guilt and regret from that decision follows me to this day, because I chose not to be open and honest with a woman who deserved both. She deserved that openness as we prepared to get married.

We drove together to a jewelry store to choose rings, which ended up being a two-carat diamond for her and a simple band for me. Then we went to get our blood tests and marriage license. The next day, on Tuesday, I called Jason Scott, my superstar at Dan Bolen and Associates, and told him what was happening.

"Can you be our witness and my best man?" I asked.

"Of course!" he said.

Wednesday, November 9, 2013, was my birthday; I turned 66. We picked up the rings, and then got married before a justice of the peace at a Scottsdale courthouse. Jason, who was like a son to me, was our only witness.

Then we drove back to my house, where Sandy called her elders in Bellevue, Washington, while I called mine in Payson. We shocked all the brothers at both congregations with our bold, and in their views, completely rash act. We had each taken the forbidden fruit, which started a formal judicial process in two different congregations in two states. A JW judicial committee, composed of three elders who would weigh the evidence and make a determination, was formed for any "gross sin" that could lead to being disfellowshipped. As a longtime elder, I had served on numerous judicial committees. Now I was the accused rather than the judge. My gross sin was marrying a woman when I didn't have the freedom to marry after my unscriptural divorce. Sandy's gross sin was guilt by association: She had married a man who was not free to remarry.

At Sandy's congregation, the elders were in such a state of

shock that they insisted we travel to Bellevue to answer for our misdeeds. The next week we went before the elders in person. The entire experience was a lot of stern accusations and condescending questions: *Who is this man, and how did you get involved with him?*

Sandy stood firm and said she was an adult woman who had made her own decisions with a clear mind and pure heart. Throughout the grilling and questioning, they never mentioned the word "love," which was at the core of our decision to join each other in union. Sandy was widely loved and highly regarded in their congregation as a pioneer, so in the eyes of the elders who knew her well I had stolen something that was precious to them. We took our flight back to Arizona and then had to return to Washington for a second round of questioning by three elders who were now part of the judicial committee. Similarly, at my congregation in Payson we went through the same process with three of my elders, which was a softer version.

But both had the same end result: before the end of November 2013, we were both disfellowshipped. The goal was to make unrepentant sinners repentant. We were already repentant on some level, but we were also now married and truly in love. I was thrilled to be Sandy's husband, and finally free of being scrutinized under the hot microscope of the church watchdogs. I was even openly questioning whether I wanted to go back at all. Maybe being disfellowshipped was the perfect time to run away from the religion.

Sandy, however, was still dedicated to being reinstated, so I supported her and went through the same motions for myself. This meant we would continue to attend services in Payson, but we were forbidden from speaking to anyone at the congregation while we were disfellowshipped. Likewise, no one in the congregation could speak to either of us. This modern-day punishment followed in the grand tradition of Judeo-Christian public shaming punishments, from Roman crucifixion to the public stocks deployed in Colonial America.

    This was how my second and final marriage to a woman began. We were two offenders forced to march out to relate our crimes against the church. The goal of this public punishment was for us to feel the full burden of shame, and thus become repentant for transgressions against Jehovah and the congregation. Their goal, always, was to protect the congregation from harboring sinners.

Twenty

Pray the Gay Away

THERE WAS A BEAUTIFUL SILVER LINING TO BEING disfellowshipped: Sandy and I were finally together! While we (temporarily) lost all our close JW friends who could no longer speak to us, we had each other to lean into as a comforting new reality. And, of course, Jason Scott from work and his wife, Leslie, who were not Jehovah's Witnesses, remained close. Since none of my siblings knew of my church status, I had quick conversations with some and sent a simple text message to others: *Sandy and I are disfellowshipped.* With that they, too, were no longer permitted to speak to either of us (nor could we speak to them).

I told Sandy I wasn't sure if I ever wanted to go back to the church through reinstatement. My concerns and doubts had continued to grow, and this draconian judgment—of two consenting adults who loved each other dearly, choosing to marry—went beyond any reasonableness. I saw a lot of organizational issues at the church, too, among the leadership structure and how things operated. If all this hadn't been enough to drive me away for good, being disfellowshipped felt like it might be the proverbial straw to tip the balance. I was also feeling deflated because I had taken this wonderful giving sister Sandy and, in everyone's estimation, ruined her spiritual life. Nonetheless, I was still tethered to the church because I did not want to permanently lose my family, my friends, and especially my relationship to Jehovah.

Sandy was not having any of that, and reiterated her strong independence: I made my own decision to marry you. She also made it clear she was committed to being reinstated, so I supported her decision and ultimately decided that I, too, wanted to be reinstated. And the only way back into the congregation was for us both to show sufficient repentance. Under church rules, I was committing adultery every day of my life being married to a woman, because I wasn't scripturally free to remarry. We would have to repent and, eventually, apply for reinstatement in writing. In the meantime, all we could do was embrace our walk of shame by attending all the church meetings while not speaking to anyone; i.e., a months-long version of a timeout for adults.

Logistically, Sandy had married a man who lived in Arizona, but her apartment and job were still in Seattle. She and I went to work to make the transition to her new married life with me. Sandy called her brother who owned the company where she worked, and told him the good news. He had been a JW who had left "the truth" (a title I was starting to see as the ultimate misnomer), so he was able to congratulate us on our union. Sandy told him she'd be moving to Arizona by early December, which meant she'd also be retiring from her thirty-hour-a-week job at his mortgage company to focus on getting reinstated and becoming a pioneer again (once the elders deemed her sufficiently repentant and cleared her good name). Sandy was director of human resources, and had done a stellar job for her brother. However, with our marriage, Sandy no longer needed to work. Two months' worth of my workaholism at Dan Bolen and Associates would easily cover Sandy's annual part-time salary.

Before the official move, Sandy made a few trips back and forth to Seattle to organize her belongings and wrap up her affairs. Then we took a flight to Seattle together to close out her life there. Sandy's brother threw us a wedding reception attended exclusively by non-Jehovah's Witness guests, a wonderful and loving gesture that seemed more congruent with Christian teachings than the cold shunning we were getting from our church brothers and sisters. It just really made me wonder again how and whether I fit into the JW experiment Bruce Benson had sold me on in my college dorm room. As I grappled with the conflict, I turned to scripture, where it seemed I had strong support from the top on my side: *He that is without sin among you, let him cast the first stone.*

Sandy owned a 400-square-foot apartment that didn't even have an official bedroom. She had it beautifully decorated. We packed the few belongings she still had there into boxes. When it was time to go to sleep, she pulled on a cord that dropped a set of stairs that led up to a single bed in a tiny room with a window. We tried to sleep together in that bed, with my nose literally pressed against the cold glass of the window. After about two hours of that I retreated to the couch. We packed the few remaining boxes into her Toyota, and started the twenty-one-hour drive back to Arizona. We headed southeast and connected to Interstate 84, which cut right through my adopted hometown of Boise. There was no reason to stop to see my siblings, because we were all forbidden from speaking to each other. During the drive, I wondered more than once if Sandy's little Toyota would make it all the way to the desert, but it did.

Once settled in Scottsdale, Sandy and I began a wonderful life together. Because we were both disfellowshipped, other than our weekly meetings, we had no overarching church commitments. It almost felt like being expelled from school: *Wait, you're going to punish us by not letting us do extra church activities?*

With that, after our nine years of touch deprivation, we dived in and had a blast together. Being married to Sandy was fantastic. We took a two-week honeymoon to Tahiti. We were both deeply in love, and had an amazing intimate life (keeping in mind I had not previously had *any* sex for eighteen years). For me it was, at the time, the best intimacy and connection I'd ever experienced. I truly believed my configuration was working for me: sixty percent gay/forty percent straight.

I can do this! Live primarily in the forty percent of me who is heterosexual with my beautiful wife, and dabble in the sixty percent just by looking at naked men in the shower at the gym. No harm in that.

What I did not yet understand was that I was burying my true sexuality. I'd pushed it down so far not even I understood who I was. Forty-percent Dan lived with his wife in a beautiful and spacious home we bought in Scottsdale. Sandy was a great wife, cook, and housekeeper, and a beautiful woman. She was one of the most giving women I've ever known. She was constantly tending to others, sending cards to people, and offering to help whoever needed something, anything, big or small. Her baked raspberry bars were legendary. There was nothing not to like about Sandy.

Meanwhile, six months into our dutiful walk of shame at the Payson congregation, where I'd been for eight years, Sandy wrote a letter asking for reinstatement. I told her it was too soon, but she was eager to get off spiritual probation. The members in the Payson congregation had never met or seen Sandy before we got married. So the first time I showed up with my new wife, we were already disfellowshipped and being shunned. No one had ever heard Sandy's voice or spoken a word to her. We did this dance at all the meetings during the week: we could not speak, and no one spoke to us. It was unsettling to do that month after month with people who were my closest friends and family, and professed to be good Christians. As the walk of shame, it worked on that level. Only at home and away from the church could we freely express our affection for each other as a married couple. As I had predicted, six months was too soon. The elders said the two of us had not sufficiently demonstrated our repentance for a long enough duration. The incarceration of public shaming would continue.

Gavel.

Next case!

Sandy tried again with a second letter three months later, which was nine months after our marriage (yes, keep in mind we were being punished not because we assaulted someone in a drunken brawl, robbed a gas station, stole a car, or had an affair, but because we got married when we weren't supposed to, according to their church rules). The elders struck us down again.

Gavel.

Next case!

At Dan Bolen and Associates, my brother-in-law Dave Mason, who was a JW, was able to properly shun me and happily continue working at the company I owned, because he reported to Jason. That meant Dave the associate never had to speak to Dan the owner. Although he only worked about twenty hours a week and would not speak to me, I continued to pay him full benefits. That odd arrangement only lasted for a few months after our marriage, and then Dave retired. Again, he didn't tell me but rather went to Jason and resigned after hitting his fifteen-year milestone at my company.

About a year into our marriage, I crossed a new threshold in being able to trust again. Despite what I'd gone through in my first marriage with tangled finances, I trusted Sandy financially, and she never did anything to break that trust. Speaking of trust, while my intimate life with Sandy was wonderful, I was still indulging my sixty percent by looking at guys in the shower at the gym. This always filled me with immense shame and guilt, and I would reprimand myself and then spend hours talking to God and trying to "pray the gay away." I was emotionally cheating on my wife, and I didn't like the way it made me feel. My attraction to men was a constant battle of furtive glances, fantasizing, and then tamping the urges back down, followed by a wave of shame for my depravity. My duplicitous life was becoming untenable, and making me do things that were totally incongruent with who I wanted to be.

When a friend of ours was at our house scrolling through our Netflix account looking for something to watch, a number of gay-themed movies I had watched popped up.

"Dan, this is disgusting. Who watched all these gay movies?"

I followed his lead. "Oh my God, who got into our account! Someone must have hacked us." To maintain the ruse, I had to follow up by calling Netflix customer support and loudly furthering the lie that we'd been hacked, which was unacceptable.

"You have to delete these disgusting movies from our account immediately!"

Gay people can be condemned because of who we are, which is why I lived in secret for survival and protection. Lying about who had watched the movies was part of that same self-preservation. For me to admit honestly to what I'd done, and go against the grain, would've been disastrous in that situation. It is painful for me to admit I lied, but not lying would have been more than I was ready to bear.

The guilt I felt from this deceit was overwhelming, which led me back to our patio at the Payson house to pray. *Please take this away from me.* And by "this" I meant being gay, which was liking asking for who I was to somehow be removed from myself. For inspiration I sought out and read articles about men who had overcome their gayness to proudly walk the straight life. *Wow, if he can do it, I can, too!* The battle for myself, with Sandy on the other side and Jehovah in the middle, was exhausting, excruciating, and depressing.

Meanwhile, when Sandy wrote a third letter asking for us to be reinstated, we had passed the test after one year and four months: she and I were reinstated, but not fully. It was like being released from jail on parole: We could now speak with our fellow congregation members, but we were not yet allowed to comment at meetings. The people who had shunned us for sixteen months accepted us back with complete love and support, and got to hear Sandy's voice for the first time. Many of them cried as they lined up to welcome us back.

Once back in the good graces of the church brethren, I re-addicted to religion. I could be an auxiliary pioneer again, which meant sixty hours per month, so I started conducting Bible studies. The old Dan was back, getting all his little happy pats on the back and self-esteem boosts that had to be constantly re-upped. In that forty-percent life, I knew Sandy was as beautiful, strong, and admirable a person as any I'd ever known. She was a woman I had grown to love more than any other. How lucky was I to find a woman I loved so deeply to be my wife! My family loved Sandy as well. People in the congregation were drawn to us. A year after we got reinstated, Sandy returned to full-time ministry as a pioneer. We were the couple who had it all: three houses (I had added a California oceanfront address in Shell Beach), a thriving business, a wonderful marriage, and a dedicated spiritual life.

It might have all worked wonderfully, if I had just been born a different person.

Twenty-one

Tell the World Who I Am

ABOUT A WEEK BEFORE MOTHER'S DAY 2013, MY mother suffered a severe stroke. She was visiting Arizona and staying with my sister Jo, who had to rush Mom to the hospital. After the stroke Mom could barely speak, and she couldn't eat because her muscles had been so damaged. When the nurses told her they would have to use a feeding tube, Mom chose not to endure that indignity. With that decision, the end would come in a matter of days. My brother and two sisters traveled from Idaho. We all met at Mom's bedside, along with my two sisters who lived in Arizona, and told her how much we loved her.

As a Jehovah's Witness, Mom had declared in the seventies that she was one of the heavenly class of 144,000, which meant she would go to Heaven and her children would have life on Earth. It was so difficult for my sisters to accept that at the time, because we would be on Earth and she would be in Heaven. Our mother had told us several years prior to her stroke that one of the reasons she did not initially respond to Jehovah's request, his spirit calling for her to be part of the 144,000, was that she didn't want to leave her children on Earth. In Heaven she would be with Christ Jesus as a king and priest in the kingdom. She finally gave in to the request to be part of the heavenly group.

When we asked Mom if she was ready to pass on, she said "As ready as I'll ever be." Sandy and I had her transferred to our Scottsdale home, where we lived on Serena Lake. We rented a hospital bed and put it in the middle of our living room, so if she opened her eyes she would see the lake. We had all my siblings staying at our place around the clock, with sleeping bags throughout our house as we listened to our mother breathe. We called the hospice caregivers, who came and took care of her and our family by explaining the procedure of death. They would come in two to three times a day and swab her lips with morphine.

During this time different JWs from various congregations throughout the Phoenix area brought food morning, noon, and night. They brought an abundance, and gave their support to us as a family. These tenets of the Jehovah's Witnesses—the tremendous care, compassion, and support before, during, and after death—was something I always appreciated and revered about the faith. Likewise, I tried to offer the same gifts to my brothers and sisters during their own bereavements. This truly was a Christ-like quality I witnessed in action numerous times.

We all stayed there for more than a week, watching our mother fade away. Each family member would take turns sitting and talking to her. Sandy played the violin for her during those ten days we were there. Despite her being unconscious, we believed Mom would still hear our words and the music. When I woke up on May 12, which was Mother's Day, I realized she wasn't breathing. As I watched it all unfold I was mostly numb, because it had all happened so quickly. We were all crying together and trying to console one another. I had lost both my parents. By the time my dad died, I had come to accept who he was. With my mom, however, I still struggled to find that acceptance, because I had wanted her to protect us when we were so young and vulnerable. Finding that acceptance and forgiveness is something I'm still working on today.

SANDY and I lived the high life for years. We traveled to twenty-three countries and planned more. We'd been to China, Cambodia, Vietnam, Tahiti, and Europe. I drove a Mercedes-Benz, and Sandy a Lexus sport-utility vehicle. She had an enviable jewelry collection I'd bought her. Financially and materially, we wanted for nothing. Sandy was immersed in her full-time pioneering for the church, and I stayed deep in the work I loved.

When Sandy was pioneering in the Tonto Basin (and I was auxiliary pioneering), to get to the homes we had to cross a dry river bed; if it was raining it was impassable. In fact, when a couple tried to drive across during a rainstorm, their three children drowned. I had a Bible study with a young man who lived in a mobile home that was a total shambles: filthy, dirty, and almost unlivable. The man had a dog named Ranger that fell in love with Sandy and always wanted to lick her toes when she was wearing sandals, or her legs below her dress. The dog-licking freaked her out, so we got canine pepper and put it on her toes. When Ranger greeted her and took one lick, he spent the rest of our time there using his paws to try to claw the fire out of his snout. He never licked Sandy again.

In Payson I had one gentleman who was in front of his house cleaning his pickup truck as I walked up in my suit and tie.

"Good morning," I said, smiling.

"Get off my f—ing property, you f—ing moron."

Then he came at me, so I retreated and continued to the next house. He followed me up the hill, screaming at me to get a job and actually threatening me. I just smiled kindly and kept walking, but I had fear he might come after me. Little did he know that not only did I have a job, I owned the company and could buy the entire llama farm he owned on that property.

Sandy and I had each found a spouse and partner we truly admired and respected on every level. We seemingly had it all. In 2017, however, the perfect veneer started to dull ever so slightly. One major life change that came about was my decision to eventually phase myself out at work and sell Dan Bolen and Associates. I'd always told myself that when I lost my passion for running my executive search firm, I would know it was time to step away. However, as I approached age 70, I was still as passionate as ever. At that pace I wouldn't stop working until they put me in the box. I definitely did not want to work away every last moment of my life. If I wanted any time left in life without work, it was time to step away.

Concurrently, trying to deny and corral my sixty percent had only gotten more difficult. I noticed that I had been drinking more. I never really overdid it, but I didn't like that I was regularly having a couple of drinks to numb myself and not have to face the music. And with my primary lifelong addiction (work) about to go away completely, the crossroads ahead were coming into full view. I'd run from myself for almost seventy years; that undeniable voice inside was urging me to get real.

During this time, at some point Sandy and I started taking each other for granted. We started having more disagreements, and retreated into silent treatments. I'm certain it was my identity crisis fueling most of it; Sandy was still the same woman I'd married. Dan was the one being pulled in a new direction. It got bad enough that we sought professional help at Psychological Counseling Services (PCS) in Scottsdale, a nationally recognized organization run by the father-son duo of Ralph and Marcus Earle. We arrived at PCS for marriage counseling with our stated issue of generalized conflict. My lifelong secret, which I was still protecting at age 69, was not even officially on the table. In fact, discussing that issue was not even in the universe of possibility. Not yet, at least.

Sandy and I saw a couples therapist together, and we each saw our own individual therapist. My new therapist was Kris Keul. One afternoon after a couples therapy session, Sandy and I went out for tacos.

"I'm really struggling with something," I said. *Oh, my goodness... was I ready to go there?*

"What is it?"

"I can't tell you. It's too deep, shameful, and hurtful."

"You know you can tell me anything."

A lifetime of hiding had brought me to this moment. "I'm so sorry, Sandy, I have an attraction to..." My voice trailed off.

"Men?"

What? She already knew? I was mortified. The sixty percent of me thought I had so expertly hidden from her. From everyone. It was all too much. This revelation ended what had been a nice lunch and ruined the rest of the day as we both cried and processed what it all meant.

The next day I drove up to our house in Payson to pray and spend time alone crying. So much shame and self-loathing. From there, Sandy and I became even more distant with each other. And yes, most of it had to do with me. When you take each other for granted, the marriage will start to erode. We were no longer each other's number-one priority. Church was her priority, and mine was always work. But also in that mix was the battle for myself, which I had concealed from her—an inner struggle for my soul that my wife could not referee.

I panicked and spent the next weeks and months trying to fix myself by researching organizations that helped troubled souls like me get straight. Unintentionally, this search only deepened my withdrawal from Sandy, who could never fix what was unfixable in me. Sandy was intelligent, so while she didn't like what was happening, she knew I needed to figure things out on my own. At best, I believe Sandy knew she was married to a man who was bisexual. But she also knew I was faithful, so perhaps we could carve out a monogamous relationship as long as I didn't act on the male part of my bisexuality. However, I don't think she could allow herself to process what would happen to us if I was not bisexual, but rather, gay.

In fact, I was a gay man still struggling to make my forty percent the best it could be. Sadly, I had lost my physical attraction to Sandy when she gained weight. I have to take ownership: I've always struggled with men and women who are overweight or obese. I'm judgmental of such people, and I'm not proud of that. I'm healthy and fit, and yet I even judge myself every day because of my weight. Of course I hate it when people judge me because I'm gay. I was rude to Sandy about her weight, and shamed her. When I didn't see any change, my anger and resentment grew. And I will never stop apologizing to her for the way I treated her regarding her weight.

This was all leading me down a path to a fateful day in 2018 when I would finally, at age 70, introduce the world to the real Dan Bolen.

Twenty-two

Gut Punch

IN JANUARY 2018, I COMPLETED THE SALE OF DAN Bolen and Associates to my protégé Jason Scott, the best man at my marriage to Sandy. At 70, I was about to step away from my work addiction once and for all. I still loved the executive search industry just as much; it was truly my dream job as it had been from the start, in 1969 at Snelling and Snelling.

Everything has to be sold twice.

Sign me up!

Now I had an even bigger mission: I needed to sort out once and for all who Dan Bolen really was.

LATER that year, it was all unspoken: He knew what we were doing, I knew, and we both acted nonchalant. I was at L.A. Fitness. He was in his thirties, and when I was in the locker room he'd stare at me while I was getting undressed. During one of my cardio workouts he came and sat on the stationary bicycle next to me. This was the start of a casual friendship with Kim Banks.

"I see you're married," he said, noticing my wedding ring.

"Yes, I am," I said.

Later in the conversation I told him that my wife and I were getting counseling to deal with the problems we were having. The conversation continued throughout our workout. A few days later I saw him again, checking me out in the locker room while I did nothing to dissuade him—nor anything to encourage him, because I was, after all, married, living in my forty percent, and enjoying this non-contact sixty percent. After several weeks, I suggested we grab lunch some time.

"Yeah," he said, "that'd be nice." He was probably thirty-five years my junior, drove a Mercedes sports-utility vehicle, and owned his own building products company. The lunch never did happen, but after a couple months of mutual gazing, we took it to the next level by going out for a drink together. It was a Tuesday night; I called Sandy and told her I was going out with a friend from the gym, Kim, to have a couple drinks and that I would be home later. What I might have still somehow believed was going to be an innocent and platonic interaction would send my life on a completely new trajectory.

We sat at AZ 88, a popular upscale hangout in Scottsdale, where he told me he was attracted to men, which was the same line I'd been using my entire life. *Not gay, just attracted to men. Sixty/forty.*

"To be honest," I said, "so am I. But I'm married."

We talked for three hours, drove back to L.A. Fitness, and ended up in his SUV together. It was a rare night in the desert, pouring rain, and we started kissing. Things progressed from there, things I hadn't done with a male since I was 13. If this memoir were a film, this was the big moment, the closing scene in Act II when I finally came charging out of the closet at age 70 and admitted the truth to myself. How could I deny or suppress it even one minute longer? I was cheating on my wife with a man. If a man was married and chose to cheat, he was going to indulge the most desirable of all forbidden fruits. For many men this might mean a much younger woman, or an older woman in a corporate power suit. For me, I had zero interest in being with another woman; I'd chosen to be with a man, which could only mean one thing.

Dan Bolen was a gay man.

After a lifetime of suppressing that simple truth (simple at the core, agonizing to reconcile), I was just too exhausted to try to slice it any other way. As I drove home to my wife from my encounter with a man, I realized my epiphany was going to come with a very high cost. A wave of shame swept over me unlike any I'd ever experienced, an all-encompassing desperation to somehow escape the dilemma into which I had inserted myself. Statements of fact could not be reconciled: *I truly love Sandy. I just had sex with a man. I betrayed her trust.* A darkness enveloped me.

I got home about 9:30 p.m. and immediately went to confess my ultimate sin. One of the things Sandy and I had pledged was that we would never cheat on each other. Living in secret and not acting on it was one thing, but this was completely different, and I had to admit to Sandy immediately what I had done. Sandy and I had both agreed if either of us ever committed adultery, the marriage was over. That was non-negotiable, and I had crossed the red line.

"We need to talk," I said. "We need to get a divorce."

"What? Why? Did you do something?"

"I just had sex with a man."

Talk about a gut punch to my wife, partner, and best friend. Sandy was in disbelief. And, understandably, hysterical. She immediately called the church elders, two of whom came over that night and stayed until 1 a.m. in the morning. I knew all the elders would convene to appoint and form a judicial committee of three elders. In this particular case, my chargeable offense was not acting out my gayness (although I knew cheating with a man was the worse sort of infidelity); my official charge was adultery because, whether I'd cheated with a man or a woman, I was now an adulterer.

That night I stayed in the guest bedroom, barely slept, and got up early to drive to Payson. A day later, as I spiraled into a severe depression fueled by my shame, Kim called.

"It's not a good time," I said.

"Are you okay?," he asked. "You don't sound like yourself."

"I'm not. It's over. I've ruined everything."

We talked, and then two hours later he was at my house in Payson, and we were intimate for a second time. I called Sandy immediately after and told her what had happened again; of course, she was devastated. My suicidal thoughts ran rampant. Kim eventually left. I called my therapist, who eased me back from the immediate cliff's edge and gave me a suicide hotline number to call.

Next I made a phone call to plead with the lead elder that I was in no state to go before any judicial committee. I was spiraling into a severe depression and having suicidal thoughts. I begged him to wait until I came out of the swirling fog. He had little empathy for the accused adulterer, who had created his own misery. He pointed out that Sandy was very upset, too; she was traumatized and needed some immediate closure. The meeting would be in our Scottsdale home, and my attendance was mandatory. If I wasn't present, they would make their decision on their own without any input from me. They had all the leverage; I was over a barrel.

For the next two days I was lost in a severe depression and struggling against suicidal thoughts. It was a black fog unlike anything I'd ever experienced. I knew I would be disfellowshipped. I knew my marriage was over. I'd lost everything: my wife, my family, and my friends. I was about as alone, despondent, and desperate as one can be. Hour by hour, I spiraled downward. I felt like I had ruined my life and Sandy's. I had betrayed and let down everyone in my life.

Somehow, a couple days later I crawled out of the abyss and drove back to Scottsdale, where the meeting was convened. I stayed in the back TV room, where they could still hear me crying. My head was spinning from denying who I was my entire life, always trying to please the church and everyone else, finally acting on who I was, and in the process trampling my beautiful wife who had done nothing wrong. As I cried profusely, they admonished me to come stand before the committee. The proceeding was an out-of-body experience, and I don't remember a lot of what anyone said, including me. I do remember going through an entire box of tissues as I had to admit the details of what I had done with Kim. I was sobbing deeply as they asked me if I was repentant and sorry about what I had done to Jehovah, the congregation, and Sandy.

"Yes, of course," I said, overwhelmed by my shame.

They expected me to assure them, Jehovah, the congregation, and Sandy that it wouldn't happen again. I knew what they wanted to hear: *Yes, I assure you, Sandy, Jehovah, and the congregation, I will never commit such despicable acts again. I'm so sorry. I will never debase myself through such disgusting behavior again. I will work until my last day to make amends for my craven selfishness. I beg your mercy and forgiveness.*

However, what I actually said surprised even me: "I know I cheated on Sandy, and I will forever regret hurting her. I may never forgive myself for hurting her. I was wrong." I paused, wiping away tears. "But I cannot deny who I am any longer. So I don't know whether I'll live as a gay man or not. I can't make any guarantees to you that I won't be able to honor. From this moment forward, I'm going to live in the truth, the real truth." I pleaded for them not to cut me off from my entire family and only remaining support system, not then at my lowest point.

There was a moment of stunned silence, other than Sandy's

muffled cries. Then one of the elders spoke: "Acting on being a gay man is against God's standards. Please leave the room."

I went outside and sat on the patio with the view toward the valley below toward Camelback Mountain. A few minutes later they called me back and told me I was being disfellowshipped. Again. My longstanding sense of depression plummeted to desperation; the suicidal thoughts raced through my mind. Maybe it would be easier just to no longer exist.

Obviously Sandy was upset and emotional, too, as she dealt with all the unintended ramifications of me taking off my mask for the first time. Everything was unraveling. I was being cut off from everyone I knew and loved. The pit I'd dug was deepening into a black hole from which I'd never escape, a place cut off from my family of brothers and sisters (from church and my own siblings). I knew at that moment they would never speak to me again. The fifty years I had served the church and Jehovah counted for nothing. This felt like a death, one that came with such pain that actually dying seemed easier by comparison.

After the committee meeting, when the elders had left, I went out on the patio and started sobbing hysterically, and then drinking to numb the pain. I'd really done it: torpedoed my entire world who were all Jehovah's Witnesses. I was utterly alone wandering my dark night of the soul. I called Jason Scott to tell him I'd been disfellowshipped. He calmly assured me that he supported me. Next, in my desperate state I texted Kim, who had pulled me out of the closet, and wrote that I loved him and needed him in my life because he was all I had. That was my last-gasp attempt to find acceptance from someone, anyone, at least one human being, to tell me I was okay before I died.

I was beyond despair and drinking heavily; I was now on a mission to end it all. I guzzled limoncello, the Italian lemon liqueur, like a parched man in the desert tasting water for the first time in a week. I went back and forth between the patio and kitchen to refill my glass. In the kitchen I tripped and cut open my head on the brick surrounding the stove. Sandy heard me fall and came in to find me with blood gushing from the large gash across my head. There was a tremendous amount of blood pouring out of me, running into my eyes and mouth as I wailed, knowing I was about to meet Jehovah.

"Oh my God, Dan!" she said, grabbing the phone and dialing 9-1-1. We both knew I was on a regular dose of warfarin, a blood thinner to prevent clots, which meant I could now bleed out very easily. I'd always feared when I was a young child that being gay might kill me at the hands of my father if he ever found out, and now at 70 maybe this was fate coming to finish the job. The comforting balm of death would soon release me from a lifetime of agony.

When the paramedics arrived, I was heavily intoxicated, bleeding profusely, covered in blood, and sinking to the most desperate low ebb of my entire life. I told them to let me die, because I was a gay man.

"I've lost it all," I sobbed. "I've lost my wife. I'm a gay man: I don't want to live. Please don't let me live. I just want to bleed out."

Sandy tried climbing in the back of the ambulance with me, but they stopped her. They rushed me to the hospital, and Sandy truly didn't know whether I was going to live or die. The brothers on the judicial committee came to the hospital to support Sandy, but did not come to see or speak to me. The cut on my head required forty staples to close. When the chaos subsided somewhat and Sandy was back home, she found my phone outside and saw a text message from Kim: *I'm very concerned about you, Dan. Let's meet for coffee in the morning.* She knew him by name as the man who had blown up our marriage. She responded as me: Yes. And then they arranged a time to meet at L.A. Fitness.

The next day, as planned, while I was recuperating at the hospital Sandy went to confront Kim: "I'm Dan's wife, and I know you had an affair with my husband." Kim was floored by the encounter, and in the awkwardness of the moment he offered to buy Sandy coffee. I never spoke to or saw Kim again, until 2022 while writing this memoir. We met, and I apologized to him for pulling him into the morass of my own struggles.

After almost two days in the hospital, I returned home. And since we shared a big home in Scottsdale, Sandy stayed in one end of the house and I stayed in the other end. After being disfellowshipped again, there could be no touching, kissing, or any other physical contact with Sandy. That would be an indication of forgiveness; i.e., any intimacy would show Sandy had forgiven me, and then there would no longer be scriptural grounds for divorce.

At home I felt hopeless, ashamed, and filled with a deeper sense of loss than I'd ever felt before. Somehow, Sandy stayed and agreed to continue with more counseling. She had not yet cut our tether completely. Later, I asked to meet with the elders again at my house. The response was that they felt uncomfortable with that idea, because I was disfellowshipped. Instead, one of the church brothers on the judicial committee came alone to our house. We went and sat in the family room, with the floor-to-ceiling windows looking out to the patio, pool, and cityscape below.

"I want to put some closure on this," I said. "Do you feel any remorse, or would you have done anything differently, knowing you were dealing with someone who was suicidal?"

"What do you mean?"

"I was in the hospital after trying to commit suicide, and you wouldn't even come to my room to see if I was okay."

"At that point, you were disfellowshipped. You're not a brother anymore. You're not a Jehovah's Witness anymore. We can't have anything to do with you until you're reinstated."

Blood in, blood out.

The cult's rules offered zero flexibility. Or basic decency. I know that using the word "cult" is the worst thing I can do to describe Jehovah's Witnesses, and even as I pen these words I struggle with using the word. But this is my memoir, my truth, and using that word is what the truth tells me is the right thing to do.

I felt like an old shoe, useful for fifty years but now tossed in the trash to be hauled away. My strongest emotion was more shock than anger. Basically, once you were disfellowshipped you no longer existed. Dead or alive, you were a ghost. We got up, and I walked him to the door.

"So you don't feel any remorse," I said, still shocked; apparently I needed to hear him say it again to confirm what he had said.

"We follow the scriptures from the Bible and the organizational rules. You're not a Jehovah's Witness anymore."

I wanted to respond, but I felt completely numb. Hurt. And nonexistent. I watched him climb in his car and drive away. I didn't know at the time this would be my last interaction with any Jehovah's Witness, especially since I was going to try to be reinstated to the church.

OVER the coming months Sandy and I lived our separate lives in the same house and continued with our counseling. Sandy came to the realization that she might be able to eventually forgive me and take me back, but only if I was reinstated to the congregation. After all that had happened, I was conflicted about trying to get back into the good graces of Jehovah's Witnesses. But I was also at a crossroads, because the only way to save my marriage and get all my friends and family back would be to please Jehovah and get reinstated. The rules were the rules. And if I wanted to be reinstated, I had to start my second walk of shame. And this time I would be completely on my own, not shoulder to shoulder with Sandy like the first time. That would mean going to the meetings again with no one permitted to speak to me, nor I to any other… including my own wife. That would mean Sandy and I would take two cars to church, because I would have to leave right after a meeting concluded while Sandy would be free to stay and socialize with our friends. We would not even hold hands.

Although by then I knew I was gay, I also didn't want to lose my entire life because of it. So I started my second walk of shame, in a last-ditch attempt to get my wife and "life" back. Put another way, I had finally come out of the closet at age 70, and now I would have to crawl back into it to save my marriage.

I didn't know any gay Jehovah's Witnesses, other than one I had disfellowshipped as the chairman of a judicial committee in the eighties when I was an elder. When I was trying to sort things out with Sandy I reached out to him, because I had heard he was back in "the truth" as a Jehovah's Witness after more than ten years. He told me about another elder, who everyone called CJ. He was also gay, had suffered physical abuse by his father, was baptized as a Jehovah's Witness, had left the organization to openly live as a gay man in Southern California, and was now back and serving as an elder. This JW brother told me how much CJ had helped him to come back to "the truth" (although their communications had all been confidential and away from the congregation). Unlike me, whose every move was tracked while Sandy and I attended the congregation, CJ had been able to circumvent any church scrutiny while out living the gay lifestyle. Then he was able to return to the church, unscathed, and become an elder over a period of years.

I got CJ's phone number, ostensibly so if I ever had to counsel another gay JW who was struggling, I could call CJ for advice. Of course, I called him immediately for my own reasons. He could speak to me because he was an elder now living in Albuquerque.

"I heard you were a gay elder," I said.

"I don't use that term anymore," he said. "Who told you that?"

I told him the name, and he encouraged me to come back to "the truth." We talked, and I ended up taking a trip to New Mexico, where I got a hotel room and spent a couple days talking to CJ. We shared our similar stories of abuse by our fathers and, for the first time, I understood how difficult being a gay Jehovah's Witness would be. CJ was fully in the closet.

During my year-long walk of shame, CJ was a positive and

steadying force who showed me a lot of empathy, compassion, and kindness during a time when I wasn't getting any support from my own elders. He broke the rules by talking to me by phone a couple times a week. I traveled to New Mexico to see him a second time. He continually encouraged me to get reinstated and come back to the truth. I held up CJ as my new model of possibility, a gay man who had left and was now back as an elder. That could be my path, too, and back to Sandy once reinstated. She insisted I get reinstated, or we would get a divorce.

Twenty-three

I Think I Know Him

ANOTHER FALLOUT FROM MY AFFAIR WITH KIM was that Sandy wanted me to find a new health club to avoid ever seeing him again. I joined the Village Health Club and Spa, a swanky and well-appointed place in Scottsdale that was more like being in a Nordstrom store with fitness equipment. Likewise, unless I trained inside a convent, switching health clubs was not going to limit my exposure to attractive men and more temptation, and especially not at my new club, which was crawling with the rich, fit, and beautiful. My sixty percent had been awakened for good.

I continued getting counseling, and worked out like a fiend to help alleviate my anxiety, my stress, and the uncertainty that now permeated every aspect of my life. Was I going to go straight, or at least learn to live in the forty percent with Sandy? Or was there some possibility of living a gay life like I'd seen Ron Mitchell enjoy as he floated by on his boat, cocktail raised, with his husband?

After a couple weeks at my new club, a female nutritionist who had done my body-fat analysis was talking with her friend; he had been a personal trainer at the club for five years and was now just a regular club member.

"I met one of our members, this 70-year-old man," the nutritionist said. "He has an amazingly low body-fat percentage. And he's really attractive."

The trainer paused and then nodded. "I think I know him: white hair? Glasses. Nice voice."

Two days later, in the steam room I met the former trainer, John Preston, and my life would never be the same.

JOHN Preston was born August 7, 1968, and grew up in Battle Creek, Michigan. His father Herb was a quality assurance foreman for Clark Equipment, the large company that operates across the materials handling, construction, agriculture, and landscaping industries. His mother Marion was given up for adoption when she was 10 years old by John's maternal grandparents, who both struggled with alcoholism. They put their daughter on a train and sent her off to go meet an aunt for the first time; the aunt was adopting her and became her surrogate mother. On the other side of his family, John had robust genes: his paternal grandmother lived to almost 111 years old. John has two older siblings, sister Beth and brother Bob, and a younger sister, Barbara.

John knew he was gay from a young age. He was also six-foot-two by his senior year of high school; very athletic, he blended in with the straight boys by playing neighborhood games of basketball and football. No one knew John was gay, and he didn't let them know.

When John turned 19 in 1987, he wanted to leave Michigan with the intent of never returning. He joined his older brother Bob in Los Angeles and lived with him and his wife Cindy; they both worked in the film and television industry as gaffers, or lighting experts. Bob helped John join the union, IATSE Local

728 Studio Electrical Lighting Technicians, and get hired. For the next seven years John worked on film and television sets performing lighting and electrical work, which at first sounded glamorous to the Midwest transplant. In reality, the job came with good stability but required long hours of lifting, moving, packing, and repacking heavy cables, lights, stands, and other equipment in the heat and cold of the outdoor elements. During down times, John was able to sleep more, work out, eat better, and recuperate before starting the next project.

One of the first movies John worked on was *Mystic Pizza*, which was the second film for Julia Roberts. John and Julia became casual friends. On one of their days off they piled into John's car with another actor, Lily Taylor, and drove to the real nearby restaurant that inspired the movie, on Main Street in Mystic. Because they weren't 21 yet and didn't have fake IDs, the restaurant manager offered them forms they could complete to verify they were of legal age to consume alcohol. Julia, unfortunately, wrote down her real birthday. The manager asked them to leave after they had managed to order and finish their first drink.

While living in Los Angeles, John came out as gay to his sister-in-law Cindy, and then to his brother Bob. Neither had any issue with the news, and both totally accepted John. From there John opened up to his sisters and parents. His dad was immediately accepting, but John's mom needed some time to process the news and blamed herself for not doing her job as a mom by raising a gay child. Eventually, however, she came around to totally accept John.

After seven years in Hollywood, the grind of eighteen-hour days led John to seek other career options. He eventually settled on becoming a personal trainer after years of discovering how good he felt when he ate well and worked out. He enrolled at Long Beach State, worked as a personal trainer, and became ACE- and ACSM-certified. In 1998 he earned his bachelor's degree in kinesiology. The next year John moved to Arizona, where his parents had started spending winters in the early nineties. John's older sister lived there, too.

In 2018 John earned his master's degree in exercise science and wellness, with a 4.0 GPA, from Arizona State University. He landed a plum gig as the director of fitness at the upscale Village Health Club and Spa. Of course, on the day I met John in the steam room of that same club, I didn't know any of his backstory. We introduced ourselves and struck up a conversation.

"Are you married?" I asked.

"Yes," he said, an answer I admit was a little deflating, because John was about twenty years younger than I, very attractive, and fit. After all, he had worked as a fitness trainer for twenty years and was a member at the nicest health club in metropolitan Phoenix. He would be a great catch for any interested woman. Or man. I did not yet know whether John played for the home team or the visitors.

"Do you have any children?" I asked.

"No," he said. "I'm married to a man."

There was my answer, and now I was really intrigued. Here was a handsome man who was married to a man. I was curious about how that all worked. He told me he and his husband had been together eighteen years.

"My husband is 70," John said.

"Wow. There's quite an age difference." At age 70 myself, one of my big fears was re-entering the dating world. I'd always been attracted to younger men, but my fear was that no one would be interested in me at my age.

"Yeah, almost twenty years," John said.

"It's nice to know there's hope for me," I said, not fully realizing I had just given my gay away. Of course, John picked up on the signal. What he didn't tell me is that he had been noticing me, and finding me attractive, before we met. When John told me he was 51, I was shocked.

"There's no way you're in your fifties!"

"It's the steam," he said. "It hides my wrinkles."

"I'm going to need to see your driver's license to prove you're 51."

When we were getting dressed, John walked over and showed me his driver's license; sure enough, he was 51. We had a laugh, and I suggested we get a drink sometime. We exchanged phone numbers. What I learned later is that John thought I was a married man looking for a fling with a man on the side. In fact, that meeting began a close friendship with John that would deepen over the next year as I tried to solve my existential crisis, get reinstated, and salvage my marriage. John was married too, and I was no homewrecker, so there was an easy freedom in just openly talking to John without any other pressure. What intrigued me was that I had a new friend who could guide and educate me about what my life might look like if I followed my sixty percent to see where it might lead. Without any dating complications, John and I were equally open and vulnerable as we became good friends.

Eventually, we went to Happy Hour to get a drink. What was supposed to be a casual interaction between two friends became more of an investigation as I asked all types of questions about being gay. After about an hour of me interrogating John, he finally asked the question.

"Are you interested in men, Dan?"

Despite my obvious sleuthing, this caught me off guard. I was still nowhere near being able to openly share. "I don't know you well enough to answer that question," I replied. John smiled; he had his answer. "I have to be home by eight for dinner with my husband. Because I am interested in men, and only men." We both smiled. "You know, Dan, you've been drilling me with questions for over an hour. I ask you one question, and you don't answer it."

I nodded. I tried to stop my eyes from tearing up, but it was too late. "Yes, I'm attracted to men."

Then I broke down and started back at the beginning. I told John the entire story about the rainy night and that I was now living separately from my wife, in the same house, and trying to get reinstated to my church. I told him about the ground rules of being disfellowshipped: no touching, very little conversation, the public shaming through silence, and all focus on repentance. I told him the only time Sandy and I really communicated was when we were in a room with our therapist. John seemed perplexed that I would want to rejoin an organization that had judged me so harshly and cast me out so easily after a lifetime of service.

"I understand what you're saying, but this has been my family since college. If I lose them, I lose everything. I'm also struggling and wondering whether Jehovah God will ever love and accept me as a gay man."

John nodded. I suspected he had more to say on the subject… a lot more. But John was also very even-keeled, accepting, and gentle. He wasn't going to judge me, or tell me what to do.

"Well, whenever you need to talk, now you have a friend who understands what you're going through," he said.

That Happy Hour session at Grassroots Kitchen & Tap, which was just down Via de Ventura and close to our club, became a regular routine for John and me. Our friendship developed and deepened. We delved into serious topics, and laughed about lighter subjects.

Without really trying, he affirmed that I was okay, whatever route I chose. Happy Hour with John was like therapy for the price of drinks, because I always walked out with new insights.

In addition to my bargain-rate Happy Hour therapy with John, I was working hard to figure myself out. I was part of a men's compulsivity group, where I listened to other men talk about the consequences of their addictions—to alcohol, drugs, sex, work, codependence (fixing others), gambling, fetishes, food; you name it, people found every way to medicate themselves—and the common threads that had led all of us deeper into despair. Marriages frayed. Health deteriorated. Finances crumbled. The details of our stories were different, but I recognized myself in their pain. I actually found the courage to come out as bisexual to my group members, who unanimously accepted me.

I had come out to my individual therapist Kris Keul, too, as sixty/forty, because I still wanted to save my marriage. Coming out as officially gay was not on the table, but I was finding growing acceptance within myself to identify as bisexual. Kris was the first person I really opened up to and shared all the dark secrets of my life, about my father's rage and all the rest. Sandy met my therapist, and I hers, during our intensive counseling week. Despite all this work, at princely sums, my sexuality was still at the fringes of our couples therapeutic work, which was all centered around the pain and distrust I had foisted onto Sandy through my affair.

Kris was the one person who really could understand what it was like for me. Before I ever told him, he was savvy enough to figure out I was a gay man denying my truth—and was instead trying to fix everything, because that's what I did. Dan Bolen was the fix-it man, and I still viewed my gayness as a home-improvement project I could successfully complete with the right YouTube tutorial, correct supplies, and proper tools. At Happy Hour therapy one night I finally told John.

"I like men."

John smiled. "I know. We've already established that."

"What I mean is, I'm gay."

"I know," John said. "And are you okay with that?"

"I'm not sure," I said.

John was having his own problems in his marriage, and at times he still thought I might be in search of a quick fling with him. However, I always viewed John as off-limits, because he was married. John shared that he and his husband had enjoyed almost no intimacy for the previous ten years.

"Wow," I said. "And you're not even a Jehovah's Witness. I thought only we did that to ourselves."

John could laugh at his own struggles. But as he shared more, I realized just how serious a situation he was trying to navigate.

He and his husband had become like roommates. When I would see them at the club together, which was rare because they came at different times, there was no closeness or interaction between them. His husband suffered from social anxiety. In eighteen years, they had never had anyone over to their house other than close family members. They never went out to a theater or live performances. The only time they spent together was dinner at night. Then they would talk and go to bed with no physical contact.

I was grateful to be there for John, to be a confidante as he had done for me. Our friendship was deepening, and built on a solid foundation of honesty and transparency. Neither of us was trying to impress the other to some other end; we both just really needed a best friend to weather our respective challenges.

Twenty-four

I Am a Gay Man

MY INNER BATTLE RAGED. I WAS GETTING MORE comfortable with my mental state and acceptance that I was a gay man. I had come out of the closet at 70, but if I wanted to be a Jehovah's Witness and save my marriage, I would have to go back into the closet. I loved Sandy as much as one could love any woman, and I still love her deeply today. I also know the pain, hurt, and devastation I wrought in our lives. I was still searching for answers when John and I met for Happy Hour again.

I was asking John how he had remained in his marriage for so long without being intimate with his husband. When he told me he had gone outside the marriage to get those needs met, I was taken aback. That's when I knew I was falling in love with him, because I became very emotional and started crying.

"What's wrong?" he asked.

"This is just wrong, John. You need to go to your husband and tell him. Be open and honest."

It terrified me, because I was judging John when I had done the same in my own marriage. Yes, I had messed up my marriage, but I was not going to mess up someone else's. I did not want to be John's or anyone else's other man, because I knew full well the devastation I had caused myself and my wife by going outside our marriage. I was so distraught when John told me. I couldn't fall in love with a man who would do that to me.

"You need to decide what you're going to do," I told him.

"I'm not making any major decisions right now."

That was the summer of 2019, and the beginning of me pulling back from John. I felt a deep love for John equal—but in a powerful new way—to what I had with Sandy. We still saw each other at the health club and went to Happy Hour here and there. But there was now a wall between us that had not been there before.

As summer turned to fall, I was still lost as to what path I would walk. One night John and I found ourselves back at Grassroots for Happy Hour. I finally admitted to him that I had strong feelings for him. And he shared that he felt the same way about me. It was November 2019 when we walked out to the parking lot. Before leaving, we kissed goodbye, which was incredible. We'd never had any physical contact through our entire friendship.

"I'm attracted to you," I said. "I'm falling for you."

"I am, too, Dan."

But John was married, and so was I! I had made a promise to myself not to do this again. As I drove home it all hit me square: I was a gay man who couldn't be married to Sandy, despite loving her more than I've ever loved any woman. It was time to let her go, because I didn't want her to be married to a gay man.

For more than seventy years I had tried to please the church, my family, and my wives. This was the first time I was going to do what was best for Dan. I was hit with a confusing array of emotions as I pulled up to our house: anxiety, shame, and yet the deepest sense of peace I'd ever felt my entire life. Just as when I'd had my first affair with a man, I told Sandy immediately after getting home.

"Sandy, I tried my best for more than a year. I have a good friend, John, at the club. Tonight I kissed him. I am a gay man. I don't want you to be with a gay man. I'm going to file for divorce tomorrow."

Sandy was obviously upset but, I believe she felt some small measure of relief, because, despite the emotional cost, this clarity would finally move us out of confusion. I knew she would not be able to trust me again, either, and I didn't want us to live like that. In that way, I would never hurt her again. The next day we went back to the attorney who had helped us execute our prenuptial agreement. I was finally free to be who I'd always been.

"Sandy and I are getting a divorce," I told the attorney. "I'm a gay man, and I've denied it all these years. I can't do it anymore. I want to treat Sandy as kindly as I can."

She was crying softly as we began the paperwork to file for an uncontested divorce. We would still live in the same house until we sorted things out. Sandy had an international JW convention in December 2019 that took her to Argentina. There was an important call I needed to make: to CJ, the closeted gay elder who had become a dear friend over the previous year.

"CJ, I'm not coming back to the truth. I'm a gay man, and that's how I'm going to live my life. My truth."

"Are you truly happy?"

"Yes, CJ, I am. I have a sense of peace now that I've never experienced."

"That's all that matters. I love you."

"I love you, too." That was the last time we ever spoke.

Once I filed for divorce, I knew I needed to move forward with my life. John was my best friend, and really my only friend, and he supported me one hundred percent. Because John was still sorting out the issues in his own marriage, I would not pursue him. After several weeks I started dating men. During a session with my therapist Kris Keul, I finally said what we had both known for a long time.

"I'm a gay man," I said.

He was so happy for me, and said, "I knew you would make this decision, which is the healthiest one for you." It was he who suggested I write this memoir. He said my demeanor changed as a sense of peace and contentment shone through me.

The year 2019 was the hardest one of my life, with losing Sandy, and the greatest year of my life, too, because I'd finally found peace. I had accepted who I was. I had let go and stopped more than seventy years of fighting my own truth. I had hoisted the white flag and ended the war. My depression lifted, and it's never been an issue since.

I went on various websites and started conversations with men. In actuality, I was looking for someone just like John. If I could not have John, I wanted someone with all his qualities. I even brought some of my dates into the health club to run them past John, who would offer his honest opinions. This was an entirely new world at my age, so I took it very slowly. I wasn't ready for anything physical with anyone, and I made that clear from the outset. After all, I was a lifelong church prude! I can still count on one hand the number of people, men and women combined, I have been with intimately. One man traveled from his home in Colorado to see me in Arizona, stayed in my house for a couple days, and abided by my no-intimacy policy. I think part of that mindset was secretly holding out for John, who was really the only person I wanted. During our regular and ongoing Happy Hour sessions, I kept John apprised of this strange new world I was navigating.

On one trip to California to look at some oceanfront property, I went on a couple dates. I liked one of the men, but he lived in Hollywood, so that wasn't going to work. I sent John a text to give him the bad news, that a long-distance relationship wasn't what I wanted. John had started working pro bono for a company called TrueTurnPro, which sold a thoracic spine isolation device to help golfers strengthen their muscles and improve their golf swings.

During our text exchange I played on his new gig.
How's TrueTurn?
Going well.
Now you need to find your TrueMan! Ostensibly I meant it as a joke. But I was also in love with John, so subconsciously I was putting myself out there. The next day John sent another text message.
When you get back from CA there's something I want to talk about.
What?
You'll just have to wait and see.

Once I was back in Arizona, John and I met at Eddie V's in Scottsdale. At our table, John moved closer to me and put his hand on my leg.

"You are my true man," he said. "I'm filing for divorce."

I started shaking and then crying. And then John was crying. The Bee Gees song *To Love Somebody* was playing, and it has been our song ever since.

Of course, John and I still had some ground to cover. We went to counseling to work out our respective issues. I needed to know John would be faithful to our relationship. And John had issues with me being a former Jehovah's Witness and all that entailed. In other words, he had never seen anyone so controlled by religion, to the point I hadn't been able to come out until age 70. Of course, because I had abandoned any plans of being reinstated, I would be forever disfellowshipped. In that way I was no longer—and never could be—a Jehovah's Witness.

On Valentine's Day 2020 my divorce to Sandy was finalized. I went well beyond the requirements of our prenuptial agreement and gave her our oceanfront condominium in Shell Beach outright, a free-and-clear property, plus enough money that she never has to work again. I have a deep love for Sandy, and will always love her. I loved her enough to set her free by being true to myself and true to her. Despite the hurt I know I've caused her, I now live in the greatest peace I've ever found.

Epilogue

Cleveland, Ohio, November 20, 2021

WHEN YOU'RE 74 AND LAND IN CLEVELAND, U.S.A. for the second time in six months, two things are going to happen. First, you're not going to the Rock & Roll Hall of Fame, because you were just there in May. Instead, you're going to see the play *Prom* with the man you love, John Preston—the same man who was at your side on the first trip earlier in the year.

Before leaving Arizona, John and I had come to a point of peace regarding my heart health and potential surgery... whatever the doctors were about to tell us. Several factors contributed to our new acceptance. We'd had a virtual call with Dr. Eric Roselli, the appointed surgeon at Cleveland Clinic should we get to that stage. Because I was getting mixed messages from Dr. Roselli and cardiologist Dr. Milind Desai, I scheduled the virtual call to get some clarity about whether I was going to need heart surgery or not. During that call, Dr. Roselli told us to reframe the surgery as something that will prolong my life, not shorten it. Since that call,

John and I had begun to look at the surgery as our friend rather than an enemy. Peace around needing heart surgery matched my other peace when I stopped lying to myself, started liking myself, and found a new life with John.

When John and I arrived in Cleveland, it was windy and painfully cold. We got there late afternoon and went directly to the same hotel, the Hyatt Regency at Arcade in downtown Cleveland. Since we'd been up since 4 a.m., we found a local restaurant nearby, grabbed a quick meal, and went to bed early. The next day, on Sunday, we worked out by running stairs throughout the eight-story arcade. One of the hotel maids was intrigued by our insanity as she watched us run up and down. She followed us into the weight room.

"How old are you?" she asked me.

"One hundred and four," I said. "Don't I look great for my age?"

She laughed. "I've never seen anyone climb the stairs like that." I flexed my biceps, and she touched them.

"Grrr," she said, and we all started laughing.

We went to see *Prom* that night. I had seen the movie version with Meryl Streep and enjoyed it. The story is about a high school girl who asks her girlfriend to the prom, which unleashes upheaval, PTA rage, and much ensuing drama. There are lots of gay-themed twists and turns, all things John and I could relate to. Interestingly, we were surrounded by mostly older heterosexual couples who all applauded it. I quietly wondered to myself how many men there might be in that audience trying to live the sixty/forty life. I'll bet there was at least one in a crowd that size. During the intermission I chatted with the lady next to me and shared the reason for our Cleveland visit. She misunderstood and thought I was having surgery the next day at Cleveland Clinic, not just going for my regular checkup. She told me her uncle, who was also in the audience that night, had recently had four bypass surgeries at Cleveland Clinic.

The play turned out to be one of the best live performances

we'd ever seen. Afterward, the woman next to me found her uncle and introduced us. He was extremely compassionate, and reassured me that Cleveland Clinic had the best surgeons in the world. I explained the real reason I was going, and he gave me his telephone number and told me to keep in contact.

In this new life I'm living, I found it encouraging that John and I could openly go as a couple to a gay-themed play and get unconditional support from straight people we'd never met. I felt encouraged that a stranger would take interest in me, especially after being able to deduce that I'm gay. After braving the walk to the hotel in twenty-five degree weather, we went to bed in preparation for the big day.

My first appointment was the next morning, November 22. They ran me through a gauntlet of tests, including an MRI with contrast, an EKG, blood work, and an EKG stress test, which I aced despite having had to fast the prior twenty-four hours. Once I'd completed all the tests, we met with Dr. Desai, who said everything was exactly the same as the last tests in May. This was amazing news, because he was telling us that I was in excellent health and could push out any potential heart surgery another eight months.

John and I arranged an Uber ride, headed back to the hotel, and enjoyed another meal at a beautiful place called Pier W right on Lake Erie. Our table overlooked the water and night skyline. I was at complete peace, with the man I loved who supported me unconditionally. I've always admired the quiet way John exudes his own deep sense of peace. He is a calm and accepting soul. John deals with what's going on in the moment, rather than living in the past or the future.

The next day we returned to Phoenix and then made the drive to Scottsdale. Once home I was feeling tired after an early flight and long day of travel. Mostly I was feeling grateful and appreciative to have finally arrived here, a place where I can keep growing in my truth, which has replaced "the truth" I once followed as a Jehovah's Witness. I want to be clear: I still have a positive regard for my time as a JW and all it brought me, including a loving family. The many wonderful people I came to know shepherded and held me as I journeyed to figure out who I was. Part of my journey has been to reconcile where I stand on things with the church. I am no longer a Jehovah's Witness because I am disfellowshipped. I also no longer agree with what Jehovah's Witnesses profess to believe. However, my experience through a lifetime was that almost every person I encountered was kind, giving, loving, and strived to do good. It is for those reasons that, despite having been banished from their ranks, I believe strongly that Jehovah's Witnesses truly care about each other as brothers and sisters. My big disconnect is with all the organizational rules and regulations that demean human beings and are in direct conflict with what scriptures teach.

In being a Jehovah's Witness for all those years, accepting Jehovah as the true God, I also had to accept that the organization was run by men. I'm still a spiritual man working on Jehovah accepting me, even though I no longer accept the man-made organization. Bridging that gap will take some time. I've had a tough time praying to Jehovah right now, and I believe He knows why. I want to have a direct relationship with Him, individually, without any intervening organization. Jehovah is patient with me and has to understand how hard this lifelong journey has been for me. I believe in so many principles that Jehovah's Witnesses teach, yet I don't think I'll find an organization with tenets that align with the Bible as I do and allow me to have a one-on-one relationship with God. I really believe that may not exist, so my relationship with God in Christ Jesus will have to be one-on-one, individually, and that's my goal. Some of the Jehovah's Witnesses organizations call its governing body the mother. I've only had one mother in this lifetime, and she is deceased.

Jehovah knows I'm a spiritual man. He also has to now understand the withdrawal I'm going through separating Him from the organization. Maybe that's part of the brainwashing that has been going on with me for decades. I don't have the answers. One of the things Jehovah's Witnesses teach in their preaching work is that we're seeking those with three H's: humble, hungry, and honest. Humble enough to accept the truth, hungry enough to seek it, and honest in our heart. I believe this memoir is testament to me being humble enough to accept who I am, hungry enough to finally find the courage to come out, and honest, vulnerable, and transparent enough to lay my truth on the table without shame.

Sadly, my own sense of forgiveness and acceptance of myself, and with the church, is not reciprocated by my surviving siblings and their families, who are still forbidden from speaking to me because I'm disfellowshipped. I want to believe that while they don't love that I'm gay, they still love me as Danny. If they're able to find their way to these pages, I would say the same: While I may not agree with you on everything, I love you as my siblings and always will. The same goes for my daughter Tiffany: I love you. And I apologize for any and all the hurt I and my family of origin caused, which was never our intention. While I know you accept your dad 100 percent as a gay man, I know you struggle with your own issues brought on by the dysfunctional home environment we created.

With Sandy, I will always navigate a more complex web of emotions. I still talk to Sandy periodically, and tell her I will love her forever and then some. And that's painful for her to hear, but it's my truth. In our marriage, we were best friends. We spent a lot of time in the ministry of Jehovah's Witnesses together and shared many blessed times. We made incredible friendships at the congregations in Payson and Scottsdale. We were well loved and respected, which are gifts I hope we both hold onto.

Sandy and I are both still healing from all that transpired between us: nine years of love and deprivation, followed by wonderful years of finally being married, and then the unraveling

I inadvertently caused as I moved toward my truth. I'm very fortunate that she and I can still connect to share little parts of our lives. I thank her for that graciousness, because as a dedicated Jehovah's Witness she is supposed to shun any disfellowshipped member. I don't think I'll ever entirely come to grips with the deep hurt I caused Sandy; that pain will always be there for me. Time does heal all wounds, but can leave deep scar tissue, too. I'm sorry for the scars I have left behind.

All I can do now is be the real Dan Bolen. And for my family, the real Danny. To get here I had to navigate a seventy-year storm of so much shame and self-loathing. I couldn't even utter the word "gay." Now I'm proud to say it: I'm a gay man, in love with a gay man. If something happened to John and our relationship, I would be devastated. I would grieve for a long time, but I would survive. With or without John, I'm centered in who I am. The reason: I love and accept who I am! I have found the two greatest gifts we can ever give ourselves, acceptance and peace, and I will never give these up.

When I began this memoir, my plan was to only print a limited quantity to share with my closest friends and family (who may or may not read the book). I want my family to know the real Danny, and since they cannot talk to me, the only way I might reach them is through this book. Certainly I was not able to imagine making my entire story public. As I went through the process of peeling back the layers with my co-author, something magical began to happen, which was the realization that the truth shall indeed set you free. In being willing to speak my truth, I realized I have a duty to share my story, and hopefully be a champion to others who might be struggling with who they are. I've come full circle, from complete shame to acceptance, and now a new mission: to guide and counsel others still trapped in the darkness of self-doubt.

WELCOME to my world, a life no longer steeped in high energy and dark terror. Now I live with an abiding sense of peace and acceptance, for where I've been, who I am, and where I'm going. Gratitude has (mostly) replaced judgment. Forgiveness, largely for myself, is now my mainstay.

I made my first million when I was 30, and sure, that's one to celebrate. If I could do it over again, I would make adjustments to my career and not lose myself in my work. I did the work of four people; I was a workaholic. I regret to say work was the number-one thing in my life, because while I loved what I did, work allowed me to hide from my overwhelming shame of being a gay man. Whenever I would think about it, I just worked harder to bury it deeper.

From that, my relationships suffered. I wasn't always available for my first wife and daughter when they each needed me to be there in different ways. I wasn't motivated to make money, but rather by a love of what I did and a genuine love of people. And that's what finally got me here, after seventy years of searching, to this wonderful new place of peace and acceptance.

Love.

A new commandment I give to you, that you love one another; as I have loved you, that you also love one another.

And to that I would add: love yourself. Be yourself. Always lead with acceptance and love. That is where you'll find all you need. And then come home to who you really are—however circuitous, long, and winding your route might become.

North to Alaska!

Acknowledgments

I would like to thank Sandy, my wife of more than seven years. We were truly best friends, and made marvelous memories together by sharing in our faith and traveling the world. Sandy, I will always love you—for now, eternity, and then some.

I would like to thank my daughter, Tiffany, who is no longer a Jehovah's Witness and has accepted me for who I am, as well as two of my grandchildren, Devon and Jalen, who also accept me without reservation. I love you all.

I'd also like to thank my siblings and entire former family of Jehovah's Witnesses who loved, honored, respected, and supported me for more than fifty years before you each knew the real Danny, and who are not able to have any contact with me because I'm disfellowshipped and no longer a Jehovah's Witness. I will always

ACKNOWLEDGMENTS

miss our love and connection, and it will be painful for me for the rest of my life. I still love you and thank you for all the kindness and gifts through the decades, and I will try to apply the fruitage of the spirit toward you by extending forgiveness. That forgiveness is the greatest gift I can give you now.

We all have a family we're born into that we don't get to choose, and I would like to thank everyone in my new family that I have chosen and met since 2017. You are too numerous to list by name, but you know who you are.

To Kris Keul, thank you for being an outstanding therapist who always supported me for who I am, and became a true friend. Somehow you knew, before I did, where I would find my ultimate happiness.

I want to thank Jason, who purchased Dan Bolen and Associates and is like a son to me, and his wife Leslie, who have both always been extremely supportive. I love you both.

I want to thank my co-author, Landon J. Napoleon, who did an amazing job helping me get this book down, and through the process has become a very dear friend.

Finally, I would like to thank John Preston, who I love deeply. We started our relationship with a deep friendship that helped me through the most difficult chapter of my life. Each day you help me apply the fruitage of the spirit. I will always love you.

About the Authors

DAN BOLEN was born in 1947, in Spokane, Washington, and grew up in Boise, Idaho, and in several places in Alaska. After marrying a girl in white go-go boots and dropping out of college to become a Jehovah's Witness minister, he discovered he had a gift for employment recruiting, a passion that would propel him to great professional and financial success. From 1967 until 2019 he helmed the nationally recognized executive search firms Management Recruiters of Boise and Dan Bolen and Associates. This is his first book.

LANDON J. NAPOLEON is the award-winning and critically acclaimed author of fiction and nonfiction books that have been translated into multiple foreign editions. He is a previous Barnes & Noble "Discover Great New Writers" finalist and a Kirkus Reviews "Best of 2021" recipient. His debut novel *ZigZag* was adapted into a film, and his nonfiction biography *Burning Shield: The Jason Schechterle Story* was an "Arizona Republic Recommends" selection. He has a bachelor's degree in journalism from Arizona State University and a master's degree in creative writing from University of Glasgow in Scotland. He lives in Arizona.

Made in the USA
Las Vegas, NV
07 August 2024

93497476R10142